# ARRIVAL PRESS

# DIANA - A TRIBUTE TO THE PEOPLE'S QUEEN OF HEARTS

Edited by

SIMON HARWIN

First published in Great Britain in 1998 by
*ARRIVAL PRESS*
1-2 Wainman Road, Woodston,
Peterborough, PE2 7BU
Telephone (01733) 230762

HB ISBN 1 85786 648 7
SB ISBN 1 85786 653 3

# FOREWORD

*The tragic death of Diana, Princess of Wales devastated millions of people around the world. The images of thousands of mourners laying flowers at Kensington, St James' and Buckingham Palace are not easily forgotten.*

*The eerie silence that followed Diana's coffin through the streets of London and the harrowed faces of her two young sons, Princes William and Harry.*

*Elton John singing 'Candle In The Wind' is a memory that will not be forgotten and the emotion of Diana's favourite hymn 'I Pray To Thee My Country', will stay with many people for years to come.*

*Were the paparazzi to blame, was the chauffeur, Henri Paul drunk, was there another car involved? The answers to these questions are still being sought, but will anyone ever know the truth?*

*This anthology covers every aspect of Diana's death, with some truly inspiring and emotion charged poetry. The poets included have captured the thoughts and feelings of everyday people that will make this book an everlasting tribute to the life of: Diana, Princess of Wales.*

# CONTENTS

## A Tribute To Diana Princess Of Wales

*You were born to fame but not to reign*
*Even though you had a Royal name*
*Your life was sad, it seemed unfair*
*Thousands now just stand and stare*
*Without your love to touch our lives*
*Happy emotions have taken a dive*
*Flowers that are a symbol of beauty and love*
*For a Princess whose life has flown like a dove*
*Your loss to this world will never repay*
*As we watch your funeral on this sad day*
*Your joy and beauty are over and gone*
*As Elton John sings your song*
*You leave behind sad little hearts*
*Who now must go on to make a fresh start*
*You'll never be forgotten for you had many a fan*
*We love you dearly Our Princess Diana.*

**Muriel Magee**

## Diana - Queen Of Hearts

*Never again to see your face,*
*No more to feel you fond embrace.*
*Gone too sudden at the prime of your life,*
*May you rest in peace, free from worry and strife.*
*We will never forget you, for compassion you showed.*
*Your love for all people was ethereal and flowed.*
*A Lady who enthused in so many parts,*
*But to all us mortals, you were our Queen of Hearts.*

**Pauline Hall**

## Sweet Diana

*Lovely Princess Diana,*
*So fair was your face,*
*We will miss your kindness,*
*And your elegant grace.*

*Queen of our hearts,*
*Compassionate and kind,*
*A more loving friend -*
*We never will find.*

*A true loving mother -*
*To your two lovely boys,*
*May they grow up remembering*
*All the happiness and joys -*

*You showed them with love, warmth -*
*And gentleness too,*
*Our hearts feel for them -*
*Such credits to you.*

*At times you were sad,*
*Had tears in your eyes,*
*We all wanted to comfort you -*
*Our most cherished prize.*

*So goodbye sweet Diana,*
*Your life wasn't in vain,*
*May God bless and keep you -*
*Till we meet again.*

**D M Jennings**

## A Tribute To Diana

*So special, so pretty, so proud. No love*
*did you hide.*
*Everyone who knew you. No matter what*
*they did*
*Felt the greatest love within you. The love you*
*never hid.*
*We couldn't see the sadness. Which hid behind*
*those smiles.*
*We saw the love and kindness, shown through*
*those lovely eyes.*
*No-one could ever take your place. Of this*
*I'm very sure.*
*You were a very special person. Who could have*
*asked for more.*

**Edith Bebbington**

## Diana Princess Of Wales

*Goodnight my sweet Princess,*
*May you rest in peace.*
*You're a new Angel in Heaven.*
*You certainly were England's rose,*
*May God use you as a rose for his garden.*
*God bless you*
*Diana.*

**Samantha Jayne Miles (9)**

## Diana

*Her consistency of love for others never faltered once,*
*Her generosity was immense for each and everyone,*
*She gave courage to those in need,*
*A true Princess of love indeed,*
*Her beauty was inside and out,*
*Loved by all without a doubt,*
*The tireless way in which she cared,*
*Her feelings of love she always shared,*
*Now we weep one and all,*
*And silently our teardrops fall,*
*Never will there ever be,*
*A Princess loved as much as she.*

### Bunty


## A Tribute To Diana

*Dear Diana, how many hands did you hold with care,*
*How many hearts did you save from despair.*
*But who was there to hold your hand*
*When life's timer was fast running out of sand.*

*Did you not know of the love here for you,*
*Those who did not, would count only a few.*
*From all over the world, if you could but see,*
*Tributes, flowers, love notes pinned on a tree.*

*Not just women and children but grown men too,*
*Are grieving and weeping in silence for you.*
*So I say this Diana, you died not in vain,*
*For people now care about others in pain.*

### Ada Ferguson

## The People's Princess

*Tears were shed by millions*
*Even Mother Teresa shed a tear*
*She died with her friend*
*United in life, separated by death*
*Riches, glamour, fame and travel*
*They had it all, yet their clocks stopped*
*They had so much to live for*
*Now we have our memories*
*She cared for those in need*
*She gave time and comfort to the dying*
*She had world vision of peace and hope*
*Her sons will miss her, her nation weeps*
*She gave her all for the good of mankind*
*Her name will live on, her truth will be victorious*
*Her toil was not in vain*
*In Heaven she will comfort both the young*
                              *and the old.*
*The poor and the rich*
*Diana your spirit will live on forever*
*God will bless you and hold you close.*

### Keith A Davis

## To Precious Diana Queen Of Hearts

*You reached out and touched*
*so many hands.*
*You made the world a better place*
*in every land.*
*Your patience and kindness*
*was always on view*
*Your troubles of life*
*We learned from the news.*
*We realise now that it's too late*
*You've finally found your real true mate*
*Now all we can do is make amends*
*Is to reach out and touch*
*And make everyone friends*
*And remember how precious*
*You were to the world*
*And wonderful stories of you*
*Will be told.*

**Nellie Gibbs**


## Diana

*One so bold and so wise,*
*Taken from beneath our eyes,*
*A fairy Princess through and through,*
*About her death we have no clue,*
*On an island she now rests,*
*Away from slander, lies and press,*
*The Queen of people's hearts she said,*
*Now our Queen of Hearts is dead.*

**Stuart Robertson  (15)**

## Diana

*Princess Diana, Queen of our hearts,*
*Firmament star with compassion,*
*Underdog's Royal Ambassador,*
*World renowned leader of fashion,*
*At age thirty-six you have succumbed,*
*Crash victim of much too much speed.*
*Lively teenagers have lost their mum,*
*Deprived at a time of great need.*
*Steadfast and loyal to all your friends,*
*Your mortal existence no more,*
*Loveable, shy, you'll be remembered*
*Funny, vital friend of the poor.*
*Your violent destruction has shown*
*How precious is the gift of life.*
*From landmines children have lost their limbs*
*Or have been killed when war is rife.*
*Ever warm-hearted you've cuddled them close,*
*Victims of AIDS you have greeted.*
*Leprosy sufferers have felt your touch,*
*Inspired to rest undefeated.*
*For years you have had your detractors,*
*Orthodoxy's followers prim.*
*Their unspoken wish you'd disappear*
*Has been fulfilled in ways most grim.*
*A paragon of kindness and love,*
*You were a Saint many will say,*
*Betrayed, vulnerable, beautiful,*
*Eternally at peace we pray.*

**Hywel Davies**

## To Diana - With Love

*We'll miss your face,*
*We'll miss your grace,*
*We'll miss your smile,*
*We'll miss your style,*
*We'll miss those eyes!*
*So kind and wise.*
*We'll miss the fashion,*
*We'll miss your compassion,*
*We'll miss the love you gave,*
*To everyone it's true.*
*But most of all Diana*
*- our Princess,*
*We'll miss seeing you.*

### Joan Fowler

## Diana

*The world has lost a lovely star,*
*The crown has lost its fairest jewel,*
*But two pearls are left behind,*
*To shine in future days.*

*You showed your love to one and all,*
*A friendly smile for young and old,*
*The sick the dying felt you touch,*
*Now they have lost their guiding light.*

*Two boys are left to grieve and cry,*
*A mother they cannot replace,*
*We feel your pain and share your tears,*
*Her spirit must live on in you.*

### Ashelene Watson  (14)

## Forever

*Delicate, sweet and serene,*
*Immaculate and kind.*
*A Lady born to reign supreme.*
*Noticing others, strong will to bind*
*A nation together with dutiful mind.*

*Quietly pondering, thinking,*
*Using her position in linking the*
*Evil use of landmines into*
*Everyone's home via television,*
*Noting amputees' wounds with horrific precision.*

*Obvious to all the love that she shared,*
*Forever Diana's legacy, showing that she cared.*

*Healing time and eternal heartbeat,*
*Every breath a gift of loving hope.*
*A tiny zephyr disrupts the flame and heat*
*Rushes soberly into every heart. An antelope*
*Traverses across the plain, pursued. . . it leaps.*
*Silence. One light extinguished, the whole*
                                     *world weeps.*

**Joanna Moore**

## In Memory Of Princess Diana

*A gift from God was Princess Di*
*And in our thoughts she will not die*
*Though she died in a terrible way*
*With us all she will always stay.*

*A Princess sent from Heaven above*
*To leave us all with a gift of love.*
*A love that God alone can give*
*If we believe in Him, we live!*

*If her work is not to be in vain*
*Awake, oh Nation and hear the refrain*
*United in her death, united in sorrow*
*But have we thought what will*
*happen tomorrow?*

*Life is short and we will need to stand*
*Together in love across this land*
*We have to trust in God and He will bring*
*us through*
*To an everlasting life, His word is truth.*

*Princess Di had compassion for people in need*
*But God is the one who sows that special seed*
*To help those who suffer from all kinds of pain*
*And the Lord's death alone was not in vain.*

*The praise and glory all belongs to God alone*
*For without His help we are completely forlorn*
*Praise the Lord for Diana Princess of Wales*
*May she rest in peace, now and always.*

**Terry Thompson**

## Dear Sirs

*I was so sorry*
*And particularly upset sirs,*
*For both your own two sakes,*
*Your mother's passing deeply stirs.*

*I watched your courage today*
*At the sad sight of the funeral,*
*I saw you keep your cool*
*And dignity was wonderful.*

*You will have many teaching*
*The two of you to have the strength,*
*So needed at present*
*Please know that time will heal at length.*

*My lines to you are simple*
*Yet my heartfelt wishes know no bounds,*
*I can only feel glad*
*Your mother's now in her home-grounds.*

*The country has done her proud*
*As she, likewise, always did for it,*
*For her Queen and country*
*Your mother did more than 'her bit'.*

*Dear sirs, take life in both hands*
*And grasp the cherished memory of,*
*Our Princess Diana*
*And pray, keep her deep caring love.*

**Barbara Sherlow**

## We Will Remember

*We will remember always the tenderness*
*of your smile*
*As you cradled in your arms a sick or forlorn child*
*We will remember always how your loving caress*
*Gave comfort to the dying and hope*
*to those distressed*
*We will remember always lovely Diana Queen of*
*all our hearts*
*She was unique there will never come another*
*And we pray God will guide the young Princes*
*Who were proud to call her mother.*

### Hugh Todd

## The Princess Of Wales

*(Dedicated to Diana, Princess of Wales*
*We all love you)*

*Diana, oh Diana what a tragic way to end,*
*Your life we could never mend.*
*Your kindness we shall sorely miss,*
*You made poor people's life a bliss.*
*A sad moment for us all it is,*
*Your life brought happiness joy and fizz.*
*But now your life ends in sorrow,*
*I shall also think the same tomorrow.*
*You were so unbelievably fine,*
*I can't think of a more sorrowful time.*
*You shall be deeply missed Diana forever.*

### James Hassall  (10)

## Diana

*You inspired us through your sadness*
*You inspired us through your smile*
*You inspired us when you 'lived with us'*
*But now you've 'left us for a while'*

*Your eyes that sparkled like the stars*
*Your laughter and your style*
*We loved the way you looked at us*
*But now you've 'left us for a while'*

*Diana - you made us listen*
*You embraced us with your smile*
*Your compassion for humanity*
*But now you've 'left us for a while'*

*So short your life with us on earth*
*But it's just a tiny part*
*Through you we surely can believe*
*That this is just the start*

*You may have had unhappiness*
*Confusion in your soul*
*But now your spirit will live on*
*Your life completely whole*

*One day we'll surely meet with you*
*Again we'll see your smile*
*And never will our hearts forget*
*You've only 'left us for a while'.*

**Jean Stewart**

## Diana Princess Of Wales

*Diana words cannot express how we feel,*
*We only know pain maybe time can heal,*
*You gave so much love and so much joy*
*We could never want to or try to ignore.*

*Diana to us you were compassionate and kind*
*All that you achieved here on earth*
*Will be forever in our minds*
*You were a genteel lady so precious and true*
*No-one we know could ever replace you.*

*Whatever the colour, race or creed,*
*From the old to the young the ill and diseased*
*You showered them with love*
*That they so greatly did need*
*Diana we know that you cared very much*
*We could see it in every move, smile or touch.*

*I hope Diana, you see all of our love*
*I know you will be smiling down from above*
*Please give us the strength to carry on,*
*It will be hard Diana now that you're gone*
*Be at peace, and be happy in God's kingdom above*
*Diana queen of our hearts and all that was good.*

*We could not have loved you any less*
*Goodnight, rest in peace, and God bless*

*Please God take care of OUR SWEET, OUR KIND,*
*OUR BEAUTIFUL PRINCESS.*

**Collette Treacy**

## The Princess

*I'll tell you about a Princess*
*Who was once called Lady Di*
*Her hair was the colour of sunshine*
*Her eyes as blue as the sky*
*She met a Prince called Charles*
*He was nicknamed Action Man*
*He asked for hand in marriage*
*And the fairytale began*
*Her wedding gown was gorgeous*
*Silk, lace, and frills*
*She had two lovely children*
*She named them Harry and Wills*
*She appeared on the covers*
*Of all the magazines*
*More famous than the famous*
*And all the catwalk queens*
*She wore the finest clothes*
*The best that money could buy*
*But she was so unhappy*
*And was even seen to cry*
*She thought that she'd be Queen*
*And sit upon the throne*
*But the fairytale ended*
*And she was all alone*
*They took away her title*
*HRH no more*
*But still she visited the sick*
*The dying and the poor*
*Then at last she found new love*
*With Dodi Al Fayed*
*But now the world's in mourning*
*Our Princess Di is dead.*

**Kathleen Lever**

## Remembering Always

Engraved in our hearts,
Your name will always be,
A tender loving person,
For all the world to see.

Anyone who saw you,
Remembers you with awe,
For those who never met you,
You were their guiding star.

Dodi brought you happiness,
In the last few months of your life,
So now in God's paradise,
I will remember you as man and wife.

**Margaret Walker**


## Our Rose

A pretty bud bloomed into a Rose
As she opened out her petals          ·
We looked in wonder as we tried to take in
The depth of her beauty.

She whispered kindness on the wind
She filled the air with sweetness
She bent and swayed in life's storms
Yet her compassion never faltered.

Tragedy struck down our blossoming Rose
Right in her glorious prime
But we'll all hold dear our memories
Of a Rose beyond compare.

**Alison Shand**

## Tribute To Diana - Princess Of Wales

*Diana you were a shining star*
*Visiting and comforting those from afar*
*Your loving smile, grace and charm ·*
*Resting now where you can come to no harm*
*Your work took us to special places*
*Memories of smiling faces.*

*The old, the young, the rich, the poor*
*You'd be waiting at their door*
*To hold their hands and give a smile*
*And stay with them a little while*
*So please remember while we're apart*
*You'll always be our Queen of Hearts.*

*Don't worry about your lovely boys*
*They'll get lots of support, cuddles and toys*
*They will remember all the times you had*
*The fun, the laughter and the sad*
*So in their hearts you will always stay*
*To be remembered every day.*

*The whole world has shown such grief*
*For a special Princess, it was so brief*
*But in our hearts the memories will stay*
*To be told to those not around today*
*So loving God up above*
*Please take care of the one we loved.*

**C Heritage**

## Queen Of Hearts

*The Lord wanted an Angel*
*So he took you away*
*Sunday 31st August was that tragic day.*

*The world and its people*
*still cannot believe*
*And for many more months will still mourn*
*and grieve.*

*She was a symbol of kindness*
*of faith hope and love*
*sent to help others from Heaven above*

*Intrusion of your privacy*
*will now cease*
*we pray for you Diana, that you may*
*rest in peace.*

### Darina Davies

## Surely A Lady

*Diana, Princess of Wales of some degree,*
*With which we all must agree.*
*Princess of the nation, and the people too,*
*With a heart of care and love for you.*
*Reaching out to help to alleviate distress,*
*To lift up the fallen caught in life's wilderness.*
*Her life often sad, coping with so much despair,*
*To overcome and win the fight, 'gainst much unfair.*
*Her battle was won, in the service nobly given,*
*Helping millions to share on earth a taste of heaven.*

### John Waddington

## Our Shining Example

*She sleeps upon an island green,*
*A Princess born to be a Queen,*
*She lived for all the world to see*
*A shining example to you and me.*

*With smiles and laughter, bright and gay*
*She stopped upon her busy way.*
*To cheer the lonely and the sad,*
*To share with them the love she had.*

*We should all remember her grace and truth,*
*This Princess gone, still in her youth.*
*And strive to follow, day by day,*
*Her shining example on our way.*

*For in our hearts she will always stay,*
*Loved, and remembered every day.*

**R Perry**


## An Angel On Loan
## In Loving Memory Of Diana

*An angel sent to earth on loan*
*Has now been called to go back home.*
*No more of her beautiful, happy, smiling face.*
*We won't forget the courage, faith and love she gave.*
*Having time and love for everyone it's*
*Hard to take in that she has gone.*
*But one comforting thought on her journey*
*Home, she won't be travelling all alone.*

**Jean Lamb**

## Untitled

*To you Diana*
*An ambassador of love*
*Sent to earth*
*From heaven above*
*They say that beauty*
*Is the depth of skin*
*But you had a beauty*
*Even greater within*
*A wonderful woman*
*With a compassionate face*
*A person impossible*
*To replace*
*You filled our lives*
*With happiness and joys*
*Seeing your devotion*
*To your two lovely boys*
*They will miss you*
*How much?*
*Who could know?*
*But your spirit will be there*
*As they grow*
*What stronger a force*
*Than a mother's care*
*Challenge that, you*
*Cynics, if you dare*
*You'll live on within our life*
*Giving us strength during*
*Trouble and strife*

*You found love with Dodi*
*A man of passion*
*Who loved your inner beauty*
*And your love of fashion*
*Your memory will always*
*Remain in our hearts*
*You reached the world*
*In its remotest parts*
*Bless you Diana*
*May you both rest in peace*
*Our love for you*
*Will NEVER cease.*

**Christine Hughes**

## Diana

*God saw her footsteps falter*
*Her task was now too much*
*She gently went around the world*
*With a smile a kiss and a touch*
*She touched the hearts of all she met*
*The world owes their all an unpaid debt*
*There'll not be another who can compare*
*The gift she had was beautiful and rare*
*Her sons will miss her now they're apart*
*But one thing is sure she's left them her heart.*

**Hazel Richards**

## Diana, Princess Of Wales

Everyone can remember, each person can recall
The special look, the touch of your hand, your smile,
It tells us all
You were our Princess and our friend
It's so sad your life had to end.
But we won't forget you
Your memory will not fade
Although the flowers whither on the
                                              place where you are laid.
Farewell lovely lady
In our hearts you will stay
Our special memory of you
Will never fade away.

### Barbara Froggatt


## Untitled

When Diana was 19 she married a prince,
Looking back just a short while, think what's
happened since.
She had two sons named William and Harry,
Now the grief of the world they must carry.
She met a man named Dodi, there was love
in the air,
When we look back on her sons' childhood she really
did care.
Princess Diana, was the Queen of Hearts,
Now her sons' lives are torn apart.
In heaven she is in God's keep,
Now forever she will peacefully sleep.

### Sarah Bullock  (13)

## To Our Queen Of Hearts

*The light has gone from your lovely face,*
*No other person can ever replace,*
*The smile - the look - the touch of your hand,*
*To millions your death was so tragic and sad.*

*We will remember you with each passing day,*
*Dear Lord why did you take her away,*
*We loved you so much,*
*No words can express,*
*The feeling of sorrow and deepest regret.*

*You touched the hearts of the sick, young and old,*
*Your presence in Heaven will give life to the fold,*
*Your radiance shone like the stars in the sky,*
*An angel on earth now in Heaven up high.*

*Please God look after her,*
                    *and Diana if you're looking down,*
*To us you were the Jewel in the Crown.*

### Edna Driver


## Untitled

*God reached down and extended his hand,*
*And took you away to a better land,*
*Up to the clouds and heaven above,*
*To look after, protect you and give you his love,*
*To a place where we can harm you no more,*
*He's given you the key to heaven's door,*
*Your brand new life has now begun,*
*And you've finally found your place in the sun.*

### Lisa Crosby

## Diana - The Angel

She walked through life, with beauty and grace,
with always a smile on her lovely face.
She was happy again, after years of sadness,
her life was taken, in a moment of madness.
No-one expected she would be taken just yet.
She had such an effect on those whom she met.
The sick and the dying, the young and the old,
they held out the hands she just had to hold.

She loved her two sons, William and Harry,
and then she loved Dodi and they hoped to marry.
But fate intervened and took them away,
never to live for another day.
Their families are mourning, the people are sad,
we have lost the best Princess that we ever had.
God gave us an angel, sent from heaven above,
to teach the whole world compassion and love.

Born to be Queen, but not of our land,
our 'Queen of Hearts', with a helping hand.
She worked so hard for what she believed,
quite unaware, how much pain she relieved.
A beautiful woman both inside and out,
and a wonderful mother, without a doubt.
Heaven, we know, is a beautiful place,
so she will now walk in death,
                              with beauty and grace.

**Shirley A Bramley**

## Diana

*We can't believe it happened*
*It came as quite a shock*
*To think that you and Dodi*
*Whose hearts were interlocked*
*Will be no more around us*
*No more to see you smile*
*You didn't deserve this ending*
*You were much too good to die*
*A legacy of love you left behind*
*To all who were in need*
*The nation mourns you Diana*
*You were a friend indeed*
*But now that you have gone*
*We will always remember you*
*Through the love you have shown the world*
*Rest in peace and God bless you.*

    *EPILOGUE*

    *We must all of us remember*
    *We are only here on loan*
    *And when Our Father calls us*
    *We will make that journey home.*

**V A Bonello**

## When The Tears Have Gone

*Numbness fills my heart and soul*
*Knowing you are gone from this cruel bitter*
*world of ours, never to return.*
*We'll never see your smiling face as it brightened*
*up our day, or hear your sincere wishes spoken*
*to the nation ever again.*

*As your body lies adorned by people's flowers on a*
*grave across the lake, your soul I know is in heaven*
*with your new found love 'Dodi Al Fayed'. There you*
*have found peace at last away from the public's*
*continuous gaze.*

*Diana you were not only a Princess, but an angel of mercy as well,*
*lent to us by our Heavenly King to be*
*a messenger for him. To show us all how to behave*
*for people less fortunate than ourselves.*

*I hope deep down in my heart your Memorial will*
*raise needed money for charities that you had shown*
*so much love.*

*When the tears have gone, we will continue to hold*
*your memory inside, and pray that your children can give as much*
*love to us all, as you have shown in*
*your short life, here on earth, may God bless You,*
            *'Princess Di'.*

**Maureen Connolly**

## Sleeping Beauty

*Dearly departed, your race is run.*
*In perfect peace you rest.*
*Amongst the playground of your childhood fun.*
*No climbing trees today, you sleep beneath*
*their gentle sway.*
*Around, the beautiful flowers, a sea of glory,*
*you abound.*

*Perfume, fills the air above,*
*Resting, amongst the beauty, the birdsong sound,*
*Incensed by the whole world's love.*
*Now with your Prince of Peace,*
*Christ, up above, in Heavenly grace.*
*Every wish you hoped for, for wars to cease,*
*Selfless, you strived with smiling face.*
*Strived to make this world a better place.*

*Oh yes! You were beautiful, dutiful too!*
*For all beings, whatever colour, race or creed.*

*Welcoming, caring, hugging, even the HIV.*
*Amongst the landmines' limping amputee.*
*Everyone adored you, loved you like a friend.*
*Sleep on, Sleeping Beauty, our love will never end.*

**Peter W P Turner**

## To A Star - A Poem

When God sent down a glittering star
To spread his love both near and far
It took the form of someone high
And became our beautiful 'Lady Di'
Her young life was mixed with joy and remorse
The parents split and the inevitable divorce
She carried on regardless with effort and guile
The eyes full of sparkle and mouth with a smile
Her love for a prince was sincere and loyal
Why oh why did he turn out a royal
She was destined to settle and finally marry
Then came her treasures both Wills and Harry
Her marriage turned sour, full of misery and bliss
Hardly a word no time for a kiss
She thought of her parents, the unhappy days
So Di and husband went their own separate ways
A new world had beckoned the quest of new lands
The challenge of new glory she grabbed with
                                        both hands
The world was her oyster to spread love and
                                        good cheer
People with AIDS or leprosy she cuddled without fear
Visits to the sick and handicapped she'd
                                        regularly combine
And the maimed and crippled of the dreaded
                                        landmine
As if she was guided by the Lord up above
She spent her days spreading her love
We were all just realising what good she had done
When the crash took her young life and now she
                                        has gone

*So the glittering star went back up to God*
*But not before she gave us the nod*
*To continue her work, we've been given many starts*
*And dedicate it to Diana 'The Queen of our Hearts'*

**D Cummins**

## Untitled

*Once a young, shy girl with so much love to give,*
*We took you to our hearts as the prince's wife.*
*And though there was so much for you to learn,*
*You emerged with honours from the School of Life.*
*You showed us people need love and care,*
*No matter what their state of health,*
*Colour or creed.*
*The evidence of your work is round us everywhere.*
*You tried to be at any place there was a need.*
*Now that you're gone, a nation sadly mourns,*
*Your vital presence is already greatly missed.*
*We will remember your tireless good work,*
*Your words of comfort and the lives your*
*Kindness kissed.*
*One more star is in the sky tonight.*
*You touched so many that you never even met,*
*And yet, we all knew you as a constant friend,*
*And in your honour, we will not forget.*

**S E Seagrave Pearce**

## Earthly Angel

*Diana we loved you oh, so much*
*Lift up your hand for me to touch*
*This world alone was not for you*
*Our tears are falling like the dew*
*Our hearts must share the love you gave*
*Though they are broken we must be brave*
*You were a beautiful climbing Rose*
*To be cut down in your prime*
*The flowers are laid like soldiers in rows*
*To be gathered up in a very short time*
*You were the brightest beacon of light*
*Forever shining day and night*
*Sadly that light has diminished forever*
*Go travel through the darkness together*
*Unto a new life, a new beginning*
*Take heed dear Diana, the bells are ringing*
*The angels are singing*
*Go forth no-one can harm you now*
*Continue to shine your light in heaven*
*Princess we are thinking of you*
*Dear angel we all love you*
          *Peace be with you.*

**Lucy Atwell**

## Diana, The People's Queen Of Hearts 1997

*Princess Diana,*
> *You were the people's Queen of Hearts.*
*Darkness has fallen now you have gone.*
*You gave everyone hope, I'm one!*
*All over the world people are sad now you have gone. Perhaps to a*
*better place, that we do not know? People all over the world have lit*
*candles in*
*hope and remembrance of all the good work you*
*have done, and now sadly much more work is being*
*done now you have gone, why? We don't know why,*
*only God knows? Your boys William and Harry will*
*carry on your work for you, as you taught them well,*
*to be like you and me the ordinary people. The world*
*had a coronation on the 6th September for you*
*Diana. The Queen of people's hearts, and what a day it was! Never*
*will we see the like again. Flowers of*
*all colours and size, toys, cards and much more.*
*People showered flowers for you in places everywhere*
*to show how much we really cared for you Diana.*
*The people's Queen of Hearts, and what you have*
*done, if only you were still alive to see what you*
*achieved. Perhaps you're a bright light up there*
*and its shining down on everyone, all over the world*
*to help us all.*
*God bless you Diana the Queen we never had. May*
*you now rest in peace forever.*
> > *X X X*

*K Parsons*

## A Tribute To A Princess

*I still read the headlines in utter disbelief*
*Coming to terms with your passing . . . such grief*
*We keep asking ourselves can this really be true?*
*Why . . . such a tragic end for someone as*
*wonderful as you . . .*

*Princess Diana . . . an icon of our years*
*We followed your life, tears and fears*
*We watched your fairy-tale . . . turn for the worse*
*Where your love was doomed like some*
*ancient curse*

*But yet, you remained so compassionate . . .*
*so strong*
*Working with your charities and the world*
*gone wrong*
*You said that people needed to be loved for*
*what they are*
*And you made others feel that you were never*
*that far*

*A royal princess you might have been*
*but even a commoner's heart you would win*
*You will be remembered not only for your*
*glamour and fashion*
*But for your heart filled with love and*
*genuine compassion*

*You reached out to millions, from the young*
*to the very old*
*You gave people hope and courage to go on,*
*we're often told*
*Your captivating smile, warmth and shy glance*
*Could melt anyone's heart and place one in a trance*

*I feel so much pain thinking of you dying in the cold*
*Whilst the paparazzi just took photos . . .*
*actions so bold*
*Even in your dying moments you didn't have*
*any peace*
*But was surrounded by vultures vying for*
*their 'piece'*

*Only one consolation is that you are in a place*
*of love*
*In GOD'S safe hands up above*

**Sandra Galistan**


## Diana

*God lent you to us for such a short while*
*But long enough to adore your smile*
*Then you were so kind*
*You left a part of you behind*
*In William and his brother*
*To whom you were a wonderful mother*
*You were so kind to young and old*
*And babies you simply had to hold*
*So why? We would like to know*
*You were much too young to go.*

**M Hunt**

# Diana

*Thrust into the public eye*
*for all the world to see.*
*An unknown girl, so shy*
*A princess soon to be.*

*We shared the joy of a happy bride,*
*the first ever public kiss.*
*A prince so proud at her side,*
*to share the wedded bliss.*

*Next her greatest role to be*
*of a loving, caring mum;*
*She expressed her love so openly*
*and shared her sense of fun.*

*Then sadness touched her life,*
*her every tear we shared;*
*No longer to be a wife.*
*How deeply we all cared.*

*She gave her time so freely*
*to the homeless and the poor.*
*Her kindness showed through clearly;*
*Alas! To be no more.*

*A beauty so warm and yet, so shy.*
*An ageless, timeless treasure.*
*The girl we knew as Princess Di,*
*locked in our hearts forever.*

**E Thompson**

## Dear Diana

*Dear Diana, so short a life*
*With more than its share of stress and strife*
*Hounded for photo's wherever she went*
*no escape from photographers, who were hell bent*

*Not all the media were at fault*
*Thank God we knew Her, through a moderate cult*
*her beauty and compassion they just shone through,*
*the mirror of her soul, Her eyes so blue.*

*Your two little sons 'God breathed on them too'*
*William a mirror image of you.*
*Dodi he brought new happiness to you*
*These are the memories I will always hold true.*

*Your death was almost too much to bear*
*for one so young, it doesn't seem fair*
*but the help you have started for all mankind*
*we will follow in your footsteps, and walk*
                              *close behind.*

*Now you are gone, flown away like a dove*
*leaving behind you a legacy of love*
*you have found your reward now and you are*
                              *at peace*
*May the good work you started multiply and*
                              *NOT CEASE.*

**Anne Jessop**

## Diana
### 'Our Nation's Golden Child'

*You were the only heart*
*that felt us all.*
*You will never leave*
*our mind and soul.*
*Loving, caring and precious were you,*
*anything for others you would do.*

*A beautiful Princess*
*there was only one.*
*Princess Diana, now you're gone,*
*a gift you have left*
*to love one another,*
*every race, sister and brother.*

*We will remember you every day,*
*by giving and sharing in every way.*
*Good Night and God Bless,*
*you are in our hearts forever.*
*Your courage your goal will last*
*Forever.*

**Beverley Mansley**

# A Queen Of Hearts

*She was ours for just a little while*
*Our own Princess of Wales*
*Now sadly, we are mourning*
*In the Hills and in the Vales*

*Nations followed in her steps*
*To try to get wrongs righted*
*Our Ambassador of care and love*
*Wished the World to be united*

*She trod where others feared to tread*
*Despite any objection*
*Did a job that needed doing*
*And she did it, to perfection*

*A Joan of Arc of modern times*
*She battled on with zest*
*Fighting for the sick and needy*
*Complying with each quest*

*Her time with us was limited*
*Like a beautiful butterfly*
*She flew away and left us*
*Now we're left to wonder . . . why?*

*We'll remember her as she would wish*
*Over the coming years*
*'A Queen of Hearts' without a Crown*
*Whilst the World wears a Coronet of tears.*

### Bell Ferris

## Farewell Darling Diana

*Who will ever forget that sad Sunday we lost our*
*Princess so fair?*
*The brightest and best of all, she was loved*
*beyond compare.*
*The whole world was shocked and sorely stunned*
*that day*
*When a terrible car crash took Diana's life away.*

*You were beautiful not just of face, but also heart*
*and mind*
*The best of humanity shone clear, to those you left*
*behind,*
*Compassion, time, and tender love you always gave*
*so free,*
*Those lovely eyes the mirror of your soul, so plain*
*to see.*

*To the simplest of people, sick, dying or sad*
*With great affinity dear Lady, you gave all you had.*
*'Though often despondent with your own*
*problems too*
*You put others first Diana - so exceptional of you.*

*Giving comfort with an understanding word or*
*kindly look*
*The warmest smile, the gentlest hug, these are what*
*it took*
*To place you deep within our hearts, for all you did*
*so well*
*Queen of Hearts you will remain, as passing time*
*will tell.*

*It's Saturday and in London today, two million*
*people or more*
*Join two billion throughout the world, to mourn for*

*one they adore*
*This sea of flowers and messages all through the*
*week has gown*
*'Midst a sea of tears for you Diana, sweet bird*
*sadly flown.*

*Her Majesty and family bow heads as your cortege*
*goes by*
*The awesome scene is of disbelief to every tearful eye*
*So silently the two-hour walk proceeds with solemn*
*faces*
*Then your cherished brave sons walk behind you,*
*in the last heartbreaking paces . . .*

*To the Abbey, for a hearfelt service, so moving and*
*unique*
*For our most unique Diana, to mark this*
*poignant week.*
*Then on your final journey, tears and flowers all*
*the way,*
*Along the last long miles to your resting place,*
*but we feel the need to say -*

*'Wish we still had you with us, lovely beacon of light,*
*That was cruelly extinguished upon that*
*dreadful night.*
*How could anyone have allowed this to happen*
*to you - how?*
*Those who caused your death should serve*
*a sentence now.'*

*Your resting place is beautiful, in a lake on an island*
*so green*
*So peaceful, so quiet, so lovely, for an angel*
*so serene*
*No more hounding, hurt or pain of this life, will you*
*have to face*

For, England's most graceful and sweetest rose,
you've gone to a far better place.

Even now on Sunday, after laying you to rest,
Crowds have not gone home, but from north, south,
east and west
STILL COMING! More than ever yet, how deeply
touched they are
STILL placing flowers in sympathy, at the loss of a
magic star.
Many lives will be less bright now, without this
shining star
But their loss is Heaven's gain, and a new star
shines afar.

Please God, give Wills and Harry strength and
courage to endure
Life without their darling Mother, whose love was
deep and pure.
Guide those closest to her boys to mould them as
she'd do
Inheriting qualities of love and kind compassion too
Their memories of happy times with Mum let time
never erase
Pondered in their hearts through life, those precious
early days.

Irreplaceable LADY in every sense of the word
We thank God for you as we ask our prayers to be
heard
Farewell darling Diana, with dear Dad and
Dodi, rest,
We ask humbly of God, please grant you His best.
Give her evermore in Your Heavenly dwelling
Divine love and happiness, all others excelling. x x x

**Pearl H Duke**

## Diana

*Princess Diana you have been a gift from above*
*you taught us how to live and showed us God's love*
*This is His commandments to love Him and*
*one another*
*your love brought unity among nations like sister*
*and brother*
*your smile your love and compassion*
*shall always be remembered in all nations*
*you have been sent from God up above*
*He always takes the righteous ones,*
*when He thinks it's enough*
*He takes them to Himself to share His presence*
*and love*

*In the presence of angels in paradise above*
*I thank God for you for your short life*
*you have been through so much pain and sorrow*
*yet so much compassion and love you gave and sown*
*Diana if only you can see your harvest*
*as you lay in peace and rest*
*a harvest of unity and love among nations*
*God used you mightily in life and in death*
*if only you an see your harvest*
*I know your heart will sing and be glad*
*God's infinite wisdom who can understand*
*in your life and in death we see God's mighty hand*
*and one day Diana we shall meet again*
*But until then, rest in peace Queen of Hearts*
*who has been a Princess a gift from above*

### Tanya Benton

## Diana My Princess

*Diana, I adored you, my love for you, you'll*
*never know,*
*Through your suffering, sadness and despair, I can*
*never show*
*That I felt the pain in your heart, the loneliness,*
*the strife*
*I know - from that fairytale wedding, I have followed*
*your life*
*With your inner beauty, you captured the world*
*It's absurd that your private life should be hurled*
*under the cruel lenses which you were doomed*
*to depart,*
*You touched people and lives, you spoke from deep*
*in your heart*
*The warmth and compassion in your eyes*
*gave hope and happiness to those in need, no-one*
*can disguise*
*AIDS victims, children, elderly, no-one did*
*you deprive*
*of your reassurance that they deserved to survive.*
*Behind your suffering, your love was endless, a gift*
*so rare,*
*Courage, endurance, devotion, no one can ever*
*compare*
*With your work on the Earth, you stood like a rock,*
*Happiness you finally found, snatched away,*
*unbelievable shock.*
*A fate so cruel, life is so unfair - two boys without*
*a Mother*

*The love and eyes of adoration can be replaced by
no other.
I pray now you are resting in peace and happiness
Diana, you will always be my Queen of Hearts,
my Princess.*

### Nicola Shanahan

### *Grieve Not For Me*

*Grieve not for me for I was lent to you for just
a while,
To comfort you in sadness I gave to you my smile.
For all the sick and suffering whom I loved so
very much,
I offered them my warmth and compassion
in my touch.
But then God beckoned me to Heaven up above
Because he said he needed me to spread His word
of love.
And so I will continue as you would want me to
And one day when you join me I will meet again
with you.
My sons I leave in treasured hands as I know you
love them too,
Give them the support in the years ahead in
everything they do.
I did not want to leave them, that was the
hardest part,
For I will always love them so and keep them in
my heart.*

### Betty Whitcher

## Beautiful Angel
### (Diana, Princess of Wales
### 1st July 1961 - 31st August 1997)

*I could hardly believe it*
*When I heard the news today,*
*How could it be true*
*How could she be taken away?*

*The People's Princess*
*Our Queen of Hearts,*
*Some didn't even know her*
*But still they're torn apart.*

*Finally she found happiness*
*She was again in love,*
*But cruelly cut so short*
*Now she's up in Heaven above.*

*A truly beautiful lady*
*Who everyone will miss,*
*For everyone to leave her alone*
*Was her only simple wish.*

*But now she's gone forever*
*Leaving so much behind,*
*But her memory will go on living*
*Her loving smile will always shine.*

*For Diana is in Heaven*
*And she's the brightest star in the sky,*
*But still the world asks itself*
*Why take Diana? WHY?*

*She'll always be remembered*
*Though her absence is hard to take,*
*But now she's watching down on us from Heaven*
*And what a beautiful angel she will make.*

**Casey Ball**


## Ode To Diana

*Weeping willow weep;*
*as we bring her home to rest*
*to the place she loved the best.*
*Our sacred flower this earth caress,*
*then you need weep no more.*
*Weeping willow weep;*
*like dew on the last summer rose,*
*like autumn leaves that fall,*
*like mocking birds that call,*
*then you need weep no more.*
*Weeping willow weep;*
*like a river of no return,*
*like an aching heart that yearns,*
*like a candle flame that burns,*
*then you need weep no more.*
*Weeping willow weep;*
*as you watch beside the lake,*
*soon her soul will gently wake.*
*Then you will stand so tall*
*you need not weep at all.*

**Lilian Cherry**

## I Haven't Left, I'm Here

Lord,

> I need to speak with you
> of something that just can't be true.
> We've lost a special lady
> one, the whole world knew.

I have prayed and asked her Lord
> 'Diana please don't go'

The world and I have lost a friend
> we all do love her so.

I couldn't bear to sleep last night
my heart has ached and cried
I never will believe it Lord that she has left and died
The world is now in darkness
the lights went out the day she left.
It's now our turn to give her peace and eternal rest.

Lord,

> She did so much for many
> I can do nothing to repay
> Apart from pray her memory never goes     away.

There is this selfish feeling. I just can't let her go.
So Lord I really beg you
Let her memory live, shine and glow.
Tonight I thought I heard her voice
> 'I haven't left I'm here'

and Lord I believe she is. To guide us through
our fears.

Diana we never part from those we really love
You were so very rare,
and I for one will always feel your presence
everywhere.

**Sue Turner**

## A Tribute To Diana

*The nation has never known such sorrow*
*Diana will be in our thoughts today and*
*Every tomorrow*
*We cannot believe she has gone from our sight*
*But shall all think of her as a star shining bright*
*Diana was an angel sent to us in disguise*
*Sent on loan to show nations how to be wise*
*The love she had so deep in her heart*
*Makes it much more painful for us to part*
*But now with Dodi and God above*
*Her sons forever in her heart will love.*

**Margaret Sanders**

## Goodbye England's Rose

*When others turned away*
*When others did not care*
*An angel wiped away the tears*
*And answered every prayer.*

*A golden smile had she*
*A portrait from a pose*
*A blessing to us all*
*Known as our English Rose.*

*So Diana go most regal*
*Most loving and most true*
*With all God's humble blessings*
*In the knowledge we love you.*

**Robert Young**

## A Love As Pure As Gold

*Princess DI,*
*We loved you so,*
*You always showed us your care,*
*I admired the way you glowed and shone*
*A loving role model, a loving face.*
*So deep within our hearts you touched us,*
*With your love, you showed you cared*
*A special person to everyone,*
*A special person who was there.*
*We will miss you with all our hearts,*
*The wonderful things you did*
*For us, for your children,*
*Your family and friends*
*Never forgetting your kindness.*
*We will always remember you,*
*Never forgetting your smile*
*No-one can compare to you,*
*Our Princess Di.*
*The love you shared among us,*
*I will never forget*
*And so with the rest of the world*
*The love we felt inside us*
*A love as pure as gold.*
*No-one can ever replace you,*
*You, our 'Queen of Hearts',*
*Never forgetting your love*
*Which will always stay in our hearts.*

**Avegayle Terrado  (15)**

## Tribute To Diana

*The lines of communication are full of the*
*dreadful news*
*our lovely Princess Diana has died*
*Oh why oh why did we all have to lose*
*the lady who filled us with such pride*
*Her elegance and style, her charm and grace*
*captivated us all through the years*
*Now she's gone to a higher place*
*and a whole nation is united in tears*
*Tears for her two sons, her family and friends*
*and the incredible loss they must feel*
*Her premature departure from all of their lives*
*so overwhelmingly surreal*
*The princes were blessed with a very special mother*
*who gave them wisdom, courage and fun*
*She will always be with them in their hearts*
*and memories*
*to see them through the years to come*
*All over the world flowers and candles adorn*
*the concrete*
*and the garden of grief grows each day*
*Poignant messages of condolence make the*
*picture complete*
*but so heart wrenching to survey*
*Now we await the day when we must bid farewell*
*To our extremely special Princess Di*
*To a lady who gave us so much*
*we were cherished to be given you - goodbye.*

### D L Petterssen

## A Nation In Mourning

The world has lost a princess
A burning candle has lost its flame
A light has gone out across the world
That will never be lit again.

You've helped the people in Angola.
You helped to ease their pain.
You touched their lives so greatly in such a
wonderful way.
You will be remembered with great affection each
and every day.

And for all the wonderful things you've
done for charities in Britain and abroad
You will be remembered in our hearts and forever
be adored.

So now we will try to put our grieving hearts at ease
for now no-one can harm you and you'll be left to
rest in peace.
God has gained an angel whose beauty can't be
defined
You may be out of sight but you'll never be
out of mind.

And now as you begin your very last journey home.
There will be a nation showing so much love I wish
you could have known!

Diana you're irreplaceable you're our Queen of
Hearts and our saint,
Goodbye sweet princess may you forever
rest in peace.

**Rosalyn John**

## Tears For A Princess

All over the world the feeling's the same,
Overwhelming grief, loss and pain.
Diana's death has touched young and old,
She was a beautiful girl, with a heart of gold.
It was a terrible shock when the news came through,
Nobody actually knew what to do.
Tears started coming, they were in everyone's eyes,
As the nation started planning their last sad
                              goodbyes.
Books of condolence were signed everywhere,
People finding their burden was so hard to bear,
You just can't believe it, you hear everyone say,
The tragic events that unfolded that day.
Then came her funeral, thousands were there,
I'm sure she would never have realised, so many
                              would care.
They camped out for nights just to get a good place,
As it eventually passed by, at a very slow pace.
Her boys walked behind, what a sad sight to see,
That's when it really hit home for me.
Why had this to happen to someone so young,
She was only thirty-six and so full of fun.
God take care of Diana we pray,
We hope her and Dodi are happy today.

**Doreen Andrews**

## Our Diana

Diana you were but a shy, young maid
When, with Charles, you were first displayed -
It was the day of your engagement, I remember,
The time the Royal household had gained
                                        another member.

On the day of your wedding you were a
                                        beautiful bride,
A treasure forever for Charles, by his side,
And as the years passed by you were blessed
                                        with two sons,
From when your life seemed to become such fun.

But suddenly we knew, sadly, it wasn't to last
And you decided to put Charles in your past,
Seeking love and affection from your 'Charity bid'
And of your hope to become 'Queen of Hearts'
                                        you had opened the lid.

The last few weeks of your life you appeared
                                        to find love
And why this had to be denied by the 'One above'
Will leave everyone questioning forever more,
And especially your sons, too, of that I am sure.

As you passed through Althorp Gate my heart
                                        felt like lead,
I still can't believe that 'Our Princess' is dead -
The light has gone from our life and TV
Never again your radiant and caring smiles to see.

*I adored you, Diana, and hoped that we'd meet -*
*And although my memories are all very sweet,*
*I am saddened too much to think this can't be,*
*But I'll hold you as a 'daughter' eternally.*

**Margaret Rushby**

## Diana, Princess Of Hearts

*With your warm smile and good intent,*
*happiness was left wherever you went.*

*You loved the people young and old,*
*this showed you had a heart of gold.*

*You were never out of the public glare,*
*this to us never seemed very fair.*

*For although your work needed people's awareness,*
*you needed your privacy nevertheless.*

*Our thoughts go out to William and Harry,*
*right now they are sad, but one day we hope*
*they will be happy.*

*You have been taken from this world,*
*that seems quite rotten,*

*But PRINCESS DIANA! You will never be forgotten.*

**Carolyne, Chas, Stephen (7) & Rachel (4) Mowforth**

## Poem For Diana

*She was a gift to all of us,*
*In our memory she will always stay,*
*Because, every day in her own way,*
*She showed everyone the way.*

*Her time was so precious, whatever came that day,*
*She dealt with, in an overly acceptable manner,*
*I wonder if we could have done the same,*
*And still made speeches, without a stammer,*
*Think about it.*

*People the world over, simply loved her,*
*Why, you might say, why, was she so special,*
*Because, my friends, she did her share,*
*Of caring for others in genuine love, until,*
*That day she was taken away.*

*So suddenly, she was gone, with her friend,*
*Leaving behind, her beloved boys,*
*So, so sad her tragic end,*
*But they will remember all of the joys,*
*Always in their hearts will be,*         ·
*Memories of a mother, a friend and advisor,*
*Of everything that life can give,*
*And take, but through it all,*
*You have no choice, but to live,*
*Until you receive your call.*

*In our hearts Diana you will always stay,*
*Your people will remember you when they pray,*
*Peace and happiness is wished for you now,*
*And in the church, our heads we'll bow.*
*GOD BLESS AND KEEP FOREVER OUR PRINCESS*
*    OF WALES AND QUEEN OF HEARTS.*

**Joyce Seddon**

## A Tribute To Diana

*One day I shook hands with the Princess of Wales*
*A day I will cherish - a day to remember,*
*I first saw her car as it passed me close by,*
*Just a wave, she was gone, on that day in September*

*But later I stood, just to see if I could*
*Catch a glimpse of a Princess known simply as Di,*
*The children in front started waving and cheering,*
*And then she appeared and passed her car by.*

*She walked down the drive as the children all smiled,*
*Their hands stretching out to touch if they could,*
*A handshake, a smile and a word here and there,*
*A thrill for each child - then before me she stood.*

*Her eyes were so blue as they looked into mine,*
*Her handshake was firm, and I'd nothing to say*
*But 'Hello,' for my mind was a blank from the start,*
*Just a word and she'd gone, but it brightened*
                                        *my day.*

*And now as the nation is mourning her loss,*
*I weep for the Princess know simply as Di,*
*Remember her kindness, her love and her caring,*
*Her radiance has gone and we wonder just why.*

*A bright star has glittered and waned in the heavens,*
*But beautiful memories we'll always retain.*
*For her spirit lives on in our hope for the future,*
*The Queen of our hearts she'll forever remain.*

**M Turtle**

## In Memory Of Diana, Princess Of Wales

Diana, you were lovely,
Not only in your face,
Your heart was filled with love,
Compassion and grace.

The world misunderstood you,
As we all too often do,
But you had the courage to
Speak out, and the gift to see it through.

We knew that you were hurting,
Deep down within your soul,
But you were taken from us,
We were unable to console.

As that haunting bitter-sweet
Refrain so eloquently sung,
A 'Candle In The Wind' It said
And you were oh! So young.

There surely is a message here
For all of us to ponder,
When we think of all the need
In the great big world out yonder.

The outcast, the unwanted,
The broken, and the lame,
You loved them all the same,
I think it fills the rest of us
With guilt and real shame.

If something good can come from this,
If it touches every heart,
Then surely from this tragedy,
We may help, make a start.

**J Lea**

## Untitled

*I said a prayer to God today*
  *To tell him you were on your way*
*So he summoned his angels one by one*
  *To welcome our Princess home*

*I said a prayer to God today*
  *To plead with him to let you stay*
*He said your time on earth was through*
  *There was work in Heaven for you to do.*

*I said a prayer to God today*
  *To pick the sweetest rose and lay*
*It gently on the Isle of Peace.*
  *Where our beloved Princess sleeps*

*God answered the prayer I said today*
  *He knew that you were on your way*
*For he had your loved ones by his side*
  *As he opened the gates of Heaven wide*

*Smiling softly as you walked through*
  *Our Lord held out his hand to you*
*As the gates of Heaven gently close*
  *We know God picked the sweetest Rose.*

**Pauline Brown**

## Legacy Of Diana

*Beautiful sweet Diana rest in heavenly peace*
*Knowing your precious legend will never cease*
*The willingness to help others less fortunate*
*and alone*
*Comforting the sick and dying despite unhappiness*
*of your own*
*Unleashed thoughts to improve lives of young*
*and old*
*New stories every day most eagerly being told*
*How much your short life touched others in*
*tender embrace*
*Just the radiance of a smile lit the gloomiest place*
*Around the world people left grievously shedding*
*many tears*
*Thankful for having known of you in such*
*troubled years*

*Pavements of London became carpets of*
*perfumed flowers*
*Laid by thousands queuing in sunshine and*
*heavy showers*
*Messages of sympathy along with many of these*
*Cuddly toys and ribbons hung from trembling trees*
*Time slowly  marches on and hopefully all will find*
*Diana's legacy lingers on in the two sons left behind*
*Queen of people's hearts Diana so gladly wanted*
*to be*
*Surely much adoration and mourning for no other*
*will we see*

*A fairy-tale without a happy ending seems so*
*very wrong*
*So slumber in dream kissed sleep as your memory*
*lives on.*

### M M Davey

### Diana Princess Of Wales

*Sleeping peacefully under the trees by the lake*
*There did our princess leave us for a heavenly state*
*The queen of our hearts whom we all held so dear*
*The hardest of hearts cannot help shed a tear*

*Whose wonderful smile will now bring light to us all*
*Bring hope love and joy as our lives sometimes fall*
*We felt that you were one of us sharing life's pain*
*A remarkable young lady, your life was our gain*

*We grieve at our loss, it's a sorrow that's shared*
*We weep for her sons and their pain that's unheard*
*Who now will make us aware of folk dying of AIDS*
*Stop the land mines, if her memory should fade*

*Let us remember the smiles, the hugs for the young*
*Let us all partake in her work still to be done*
*Part of her lives that's in her two wonderful sons*
*The nation rises a last goodbye your race is won*

### A S Flack

## RIP Princess Diana

*Diana you will be*
*Sadly missed,*
*Through all those lives*
*You touched and kissed.*
*Diana you could never*
*Be replaced,*
*Through all those times*
*In life you faced.*

*You were an inspiration*
*Through your charity work,*
*Even though you died that*
*Morning in your Merc.*
*With Dodi in the car you*
*Cared,*
*Your last week with him you*
*Shared.*

*You died on the day of*
*Rest,*
*The press no more will*
*Be a pest.*
*When you were a girl*
*You were very shy,*
*Now that's gone we shall*
*All cry.*

*You were bubbly, caring*
*Charmful and witty,*
*Not to mention you were*
*Extremely pretty.*
*Delicate, graceful and*
*Incredibly smart,*
*These are the features that*
*Make the Queen of Hearts.*

**Dawn Martin (12)**

## Diana

*I look up at the sky*
*and ask myself why oh why*
*It was so unfair you had to die*
*the whole nation they did cry*
*It seemed so unreal*
*I think everyone would feel*
*that you deserved a long and happy life*
*to be free of trouble and strife*
*Your lovely sons are very sad*
*but one thing makes me glad*
*You now have the peace you deserve*
*memories of you we will preserve*
*although you are far away*
*in our hearts you will stay*
*Sleep well, Princess Diana*
*AMEN*

**Donna Holmes**

## My Inspiration!

*I lay awake in bed tonight*
*and felt the urge that I should write*
*one thousand words are in my head*
*but most of all the words 'Not dead'*

*This is one that has come to me*
*although I know not what the words*
*will be.*
*I seem to be full of fire*
*I do not slow, I do not tire*
*I feel so alive and full of drive*
*I do not know whose words are these*
*I just feel full of sense to please*
*I cannot stop, I do not want to*
*In Diana's memory I promise not to.*

*Could this be where my fate lies?*
*To see the world through Di's eyes*
*for I now too*
*feel the yearning*
*to show I care,*
*to love and be warming*
*and once I can accomplish these*
*then I too,*
*will feel the joy to please.*

*I wonder why she's chosen me*
*in my soul she seems to be*
*I have never felt so inspired,*
*to write these words - I do not tire*
*could she somehow be telling me*
*now that her spirit has been set free*
*I feel so close, I cannot describe*
*the words that are floating around inside*
*I feel a great urge to pass on these,*
*and ask you to listen if you please!*

**C L Brownless**


## Unitled

*God misplaced an angel,*
*to earth she did stray.*
*Became a fairy princess,*
*her magic to display.*
*She taught us all a new song,*
*love neighbour as thyself.*
*Greedy hands abused her,*
*to enhance their wealth.*
*She cried out to heaven,*
*God took her by the hand.*
*He dried her tears, healed the pain*
*then he took command.*
*God flew her back to heaven,*
*we on earth bowed down.*
*God placed upon her platinum head*
*a well earned golden crown.*

**L D McLellan**

## Diana

*The days go on in sadness, yet,*
*Our lives they must go on,*
*To cherish our dear Princess,*
*Whose face was true and shone.*

*Her life was always hectic*
*With plenty much to do*
*Caring for the weak and sick*
*Princes William and Harry too.*

*We sit, stare and listen*
*To all that is said and done*
*Diana will always glisten*
*We can't believe she's gone.*

*One day we'll all meet again*
*With happiness and rejoice*
*When God does take away our pain*
*We'll hear her gentle voice.*

*Diana was a mother*
*And a sister too*
*She will always be remembered*
*By folk like me and you.*

*When we have our private thoughts*
*Each night and every day*
*Let us all remember*
*Diana showed us the way.*

*We all did love her dearly*
*She clearly was the best*
*We all mean this sincerely*
*Our Princess may you rest.*

**Sammy Hagar and children**
**Tina, Tanya, Tara, Timothy and Tamara**


### Tribute To Lady Diana

*One short spell of happiness.*
*One brief spell at play.*
*Her tragic life came to an end,*
*On that eventful day.*

*There was an understanding,*
*In life she played her part.*
*The things that she did best,*
*Came straight, right from the heart.*

*Hers was a life of sorrow,*
*And one of kindly deeds.*
*The people took her to their hearts,*
*And she fulfilled their needs.*

*Although she was in public life,*
*She walked through life alone.*
*Her life so short came to an end,*
*Now she's safely home.*

**Mary Murphy**

## Kensington Revisited

*(A fond remembrance of Diana, Princess of Wales 1961-1997)*

*We took our American friends back to*
*Kensington Palace that day in May.*
*Then to tea at the Orangery.*
*It was all so very British.*

*A leisurely stroll through the gardens*
*In the heat of late afternoon.*
*Back on the main road our steps*
*Quickened.*

*We saw two outriders, a*
*Large black car was moving very slowly.*
*She bent forward. Her smile and wave*
*Was just for the four of us.*

*A double take, suddenly we realised this was*
*Our own princess, truly a vision of loveliness,*
*Graceful and every inch the*
*Embodiment of royalty.*

*A gasp of recognition and*
*Joyfully we waved back.*
*Our step was lighter for*
*This brief encounter.*
*The memory lingers on.*

*Now she has gone to her Maker.*
*The whole world is saddened for her*
*Tragic passing. Would the outriders had*
*Been with her in Paris that fateful night.*

*Two boys have lost*
*Their loving wonderful mother.*
*Let us hope that her pathetic critics realise*
*How much, and how often, they debased our*
*Priceless, National Treasure.*

**Hilary Moore**

## Diana

*God lent us an angel*
*Just for a little while.*
*To show us how to love and care*
*She made the people smile.*

*Diana set a shining example*
*Of how people should really be.*
*To love and share and care*
*And hug definitely.*

*So she's done her work here on earth*
*And made it a better place*
*Now God has taken her home*
*Because he needed her more*
*But she's left us two wonderful princes*
*Whom the nation adores*

*Rest peacefully our princess*
*Your people will watch over them.*

**Julia M Powell**

## Tribute To Diana Princess Of Wales

*She showed the world*
*The way to care,*
*To help another and -*
*Their troubles to share.*
*She gave love to others*
*Who she felt were in need.*
*Such depth of feeling*
*In her eyes you could read.*
*Love is a thing -*
*No amount of money can buy,*
*It costs nothing to give -*
*If we all try.*
*Maybe the world can learn*
*From her tragic loss,*
*To give of oneself and -*
*Not consider the cost.*
*No one can ever take her place,*
*Most of us will remember*
*Her lovely face.*
*Her tender smile, her loving touch.*
*This world will miss her -*
*Very much.*

## Alma A Dodds

## Diana, Our Princess Of Wales

*It seemed that she had everything,*
*To the great big world outside,*
*The country girl who won the heart of a prince,*
*Then became his blushing bride.*

*The simple things in life, are what*
*Meant the most to her,*
*Her beloved family, her privacy,*
*Various charities and the poor.*

*She never really cared*
*For her riches or her wealth,*
*But more for those without a home,*
*Those less fortunate, or in bad health.*

*She won the hearts of everyone,*
*From the youngest to the old,*
*Now, how much we all will miss her,*
*Never can be told.*

*For on that fateful night,*
*We lost her, her chauffeur and her friend,*
*But one as elegant, as beautiful as her,*
*The world will never see again.*

*Though with Dodi, she never lived*
*To fulfil that fairy tale,*
*We will always fondly remember and love,*
*Diana, our Princess of Wales.*

**Lorraine O'Shea**

## Diana - Reflections

*Born to high estate she seemed to wear privilege*
*as a casual garment without display,*
*Moving among her fellows, content to share the*
*common birthright of humanity.*
*Her smile dissolved barriers.*
*Children clung to her and the rejected felt*
*reinstated by her touch.*
*Folk were at ease with her.*
*In her company the tongue-tied found words and*
*the inarticulate needed none*
*For her intuition read the tale of pain in a troubled*
*face.*
*She understood.*
*Sadness and uncertainty were no strangers to her.*
*Had she known loneliness, longing for the comfort*
*of a mother's arms, the sympathetic ear or word*
*of wise advice?*
*Perhaps,*
*The restraints of royalty bore heavily upon her.*
*May not the exotic bird, aviary reared, look*
*sometimes with longing at the sparrows scratching*
*in the dust outside?*
*How much more the wild bird caged?*
*Self-wounding, she had beat her frail wings against*
*the rigid bars of protocol.*
*The glare of spotlights troubled her and she*
*sought escape.*
*The hunters' nets closed in on her seeking to entrap,*
*To hold her in cruel exposure.*
*The crowds surged forward, seeking booty.*
*They who fed on scandal as maggots on rotting*
*flesh did not mean to harm her.*

'Father forgive them, for they knew not what
they did'.
She was young and made mistakes.
The hasty word or ill-conceived venture brought
stinging rebuke.
Of course she did wrong - as who does not?
Leave judgement to the All-Seeing One.
Perhaps her very fallibility endeared her to a
stumbling generation,
One which had torn down life's signposts in the
name of freedom,
Giving to the young freedom to lose their way.

For a while she lost hers.
Then the compass of her heart directed her.
She would become a voice to the voiceless, a
champion of those who could not help themselves.

Perceiving her goal she advanced with fervour
and courage.
She could not know how short would be her time.
How sadly short!
Short but enough.
Enough to wake some flicker of awareness -
of duty to those so long ignored.

Hold fast the vision now!
Keep faith.
Let not rank weeds of apathy obscure the trail
she blazed.
Follow the course.
Build on her beginnings.
Therein, perchance, we may build her memorial.

**V E Godfrey**

## Rose Of England

In the garden of Althorp House
Lies a beautiful English rose,
The wind and the rain, caress her,
As she sleeps in sweet repose.

For Diana was a princess
Her qualities were rare
Her caring ways and compassion
Were everyone's to share.

Although we never met her
Overwhelmed with grief we are
No-one can ever replace
That bright and shining star.

You had so much to give us
You taught us to understand
What the meaning of true love is
To give and not demand.

We will remember the day we lost you
It was such a tragic day
You had to die, to show men
How to change their ways.

So sleep on dear Princess
In the garden you loved so dear
And when the rain falls upon you
It is angels shedding tears.

**Mary Seddon**

## Epitaph To Diana Princess Of Wales

*Love thy neighbour as thyself*
*as Diana sought to do.*
*Her loving smile and warm compassion*
*helped so many to pull through.*

*Thank God for giving us Diana,*
*the un-crowned 'Queen of our hearts';*
*She gave of herself magnanimously,*
*inspiring others to play their part.*

*Diana enriched our lives immeasurably;*
*She died needlessly due to man's greed.*
*Let us all work to honour her memory*
*by reaching out to help those most in need.*

*Without doubt a humanitarian,*
*loving mother, an ambassador for peace;*
*Diana, in eternal tribute,*
*may we all strive your goals to reach.*

**Malcolm F Andrews**

## Shining Star

*Because of everything you did endeavour,*
*you will be in our hearts forever,*
*and with all the love you gave,*
*and all the hearts you saved,*
*you shone like a star in the sky,*
*but even though we try, not all can say goodbye.*

**Rebecca Dobb  (14)**

## Diana - A Special Princess

*It was the thirty first of August*
*Nineteen ninety seven*
*The Lord decided he would take Diana*
*Up to heaven.*
*The timing seemed so tragic, for once she seemed*
*So happy,*
*Finding strength from her new love,*
*A man she knew as Dodi.*
*He also died and now the two are joined as one*
*In soul,*
*No-one can hurt or tarnish them,*
*No more lies can be told.*
*Diana touched the hearts of each and*
*Everyone she met,*
*Giving love, compassion that no-one will forget.*
*Making friends with all no matter what their*
*Race or breed,*
*Searching out the homeless with so many mouths*
*To feed.*
*The young, the old, the sick, the well,*
*No matter who they were,*
*She had a place for all of them,*
*A place in her heart to share.*
*Goodbye Diana from all of us may you enjoy*
*Your special love,*
*As you shine down, the brightest star,*
*Shine down from up above.*

**Janette Halliday**

## Diana, Princess Of Wales

*Diana, you were beautiful in every possible way,*
*God in his wisdom, took you away from us today,*
*we just cannot believe it, you are missed so much,*
*a caring person, everyone you loved and touched,*
*birds no longer sing, and the sun no longer shines,*
*all the ones you have loved, that are left behind,*
*your gentle hands have helped to heal our wounds,*
*we all mourn your passing, you have left us*
*too soon,*
*Diana, Princess of Wales, loved her sons with pride,*
*with all the love and affection she had inside,*
*heaven has another angel, to outshine all the others,*
*an example to us all 'Queen of Hearts',*
*a loving mother,*
*our hearts go out to William and Harry,*
*from now on,*
*Diana was adored by all, but now,*
*sadly, you are gone.*

### Josephine Elliott


## A Tribute To Diana

*Your smile was like the sunshine bursting through on a rainy day.*
*Your smile was for all the children to help ease their pain away.*

*You gave your time so willingly, fighting for what you believed.*
*Though people made false promises you were never once deceived.*

*Your work will keep on growing with every passing day.*
*Although your smile has gone for ever,*
*In our hearts you will always stay.*

### Louise O'Neill

## The Gift

Out of the sorrow
And in your hearts
'Your mum and you'
Will never part

Your mum
Had that gift
To make you smile
When you were
Sad and lonely,

And gave her love
And heart to you only,

The world
Was a better place
For her
Saving grace.

William and Harry,
In life
You will never part.
God bless.

**Bill Crossan**

## Babies

*Shining like the stars above,*
*She takes your hand in her glove,*
*In golden light, with eyes so bright*
*Her babies cry all through the night*

*Our Princess Diana, Queen of Hearts far and wide*
*Take our love and tears into the tide*
*The world has lost one so bright*
*And her babies cry all through the night*

*Remember how she held your hands,*
*Warm and in her glove*
*Remember her and share the love*
*Shining down from up above.*

### Natasha De Sousa

## For Diana - The Queen That Never Was

*As I gaze at the darkened skies,*
*I see a lone star shining so bright,*
*Jesus has welcomed our princess this night,*
*Diana was so loyal, so loving, so kind,*
*Helping the needy as much as she could,*
*Fulfilling her dreams, yet taken from us,*
*So soon we all know,*
*A short time is better, than no time at all,*
*I now pray for you, with all of my love,*
*Diana I miss you and remember,*
*You'll always be my Queen of Hearts,*
*So rest in peace with the angels above.*

### Carl Ball

## Queen Of Hearts
*(In memory of a true princess)*

*Oh sweet Lord on high above*
*Why did our angel die*
*Show her your eternal love*
*And wipe our tears dry*

*When all the world is crying*
*And it is for you they weep*
*You gave them dignity in dying*
*And joined them in their sleep*

*And as you walk through broken dreams*
*While other children cry*
*You will hear their frightened screams*
*And wipe their tears dry*

*Goodbye my lovely, goodnight God bless*
*You stole our hearts away*
*Those laughing eyes and tenderness*
*For innocents to play*

*I will always walk with thee*
*Through all life's weary trials*
*Whilst thou always walk with me*
*Those dark and lonely miles*

*Goodnight, God bless my sweet princess*
*You've left that we might start*
*All bathed in grief's togetherness*
*DIANA, our Queen of Hearts*

**R Finch**

## Thoughts Of A Grandma
## 10am on 31.8.97.

*The morning star has been extinguished!*
*A glowing light, a beacon bright,*
*A shining example of human warmth*
*And love - is no more!*
*She was saintly, ordinary, royal, so popular*
*Beloved, extraordinary, ambassador and mother -*
*Such a good mother -*
*Mother of a future king and his brother.*
*Now she has gone - so suddenly.*
*A car crash in Paris - chased by the Paparazzi*
*On seven motorbikes!*
*Terrible! Criminal! Horrendous tragedy!*
*Incomprehensible!*
*A nation in shock - why?*
*The grief is unbearable -*
*World-wide disbelief -*
*International despair -*
*Personal - her loss is so personal.*
*My princess will be missed forever,*
*I am numb -*
*I weep for Diana*
*I weep for her boys*

**Pauline Andrews**

## Untitled

*Out is the fire, out is the flame*
*Can the world ever be the same again*
*Her beauty, her youth, compassion and care*
*The way that she loved, beyond compare.*
*A daughter, a sister, a mother, once a wife*
*Special indeed to have touched a life*
*Was happiness for her ever to be*
*Apart from her boys, her immediate family*
*Then holidays, love, a meal at the Ritz*
*Off into the night, she loved him to bits*
*A surge of power, a flash of light,*
*An error of judgement, DIANA, goodnight.*

### Valerie Breithaupt

## Diana

*You were always there Diana*
*With the people who needed care Diana*
*You were always thinking Diana*
*Of the people you could help Diana*
*In far away countries East or West.*
*You tried your hardest to do your best.*
*Your two lovely boys Harry and Wills*
*To them and us the world stood still*
*We prayed and we cried*
*When you were taken away.*
*But in our hearts you will always stay.*
*So when the world stops crying*
*Loving and giving*
*That's when the world will stop living.*

### F M Kitching

## Do Not Cry For Me

*My dear people, do not cry for me,*
*now that I have gone.*
*But, do as you saw me do,*
*to help my work live on.*
*If anyone is in despair,*
*put your arms around them,*
*show them that you care.*

*Words do very little for those in distress,*
*Actions are much better, give a sweet caress*
*The love that you showed me,*
*share with others, make them free.*
*Just a small gesture, a touch, a smile, a kiss*
*For those who have never had it,*
*it is pure bliss.*

*In my heart you will all remain,*
*Please don't let my work be in vain.*

**Lesley Lister**


## The Sorrow Of Two Princes

*Two princes left behind to grieve*
*the passing of their mother*
*must now stand tall and brave and strong*
*and comfort one another.*

*And I believe she'll stay with them -*
*her spirit's very strong -*
*and guide them gently on along*
*campaigns to end what's cruel and wrong!*

**Patricia Tilling**

## Diana - Our Queen Of Hearts

*One rainy Sunday in August*
*I heard that you had died*
*My daughter told me the sad news,*
*In total shock and disbelief,*
*We comforted each other and cried*
*No more of your loving smile*
*Or those lovely blue eyes*
*We will all miss your gentle touch*
*Your voice, to ease a baby's cries.*
*You were an inspiration*
*To all people far and wide.*
*But deep down 'Diana'*
*Your own pain, you tried to hide.*
*Finally you met happiness with Dodi*
*Your life was looking bright*
*Then God went and took away*
*Our only shining light.*
*God bless and keep you both in his care.*
*For two very special people like these,*
*Are very, very rare.*

*Goodnight, God bless*
*Love,*

**Rose, Samantha and Stacey**

## Simply The Best

*As the nation unites to count the cost,*
*A charming lady it has lost.*
*Diana full of grace and charm,*          ·
*To the people she did no harm.*

*She travelled to so many lands,*
*She shook the leper by the hand.*
*To many people she gave them a hug,*
*The little ones her coat did tug.*

*She was showered with so many flowers,*
*She saw so many people in sunshine and showers.*
*We saw the sunshine in your smile,*
*As you stopped to chat awhile.*

*,And now as Diana is laid to rest*
*We say Diana you were simply the best.*
*You brought us much happiness and many joys,*
*We pray God will take care of Diana's boys.*

### David Reynoldson

## Untitled

*Oh God, you've taken our Diana*
*And what's the reason why?*
*She's done such wonders in this world*
*And now you've let her die,*
*There must be some good reason*
*Why you need our princess there*
*Perhaps you want an angel*
*To give her love elsewhere!*

### Ronald Waller

## To Diana With Love

As she lay in peace
The world, we mourn
Her goodness and kindness
From us was torn.

She dared to be different
But kept her grace and charm
Tried to rid the world of disaster
And protect us from harm.

A natural beauty
Born with class
A saint among royals
She loved with her heart.

She was the nation's friend
Brave and strong
We still love her
Although she's gone.

No words can describe
What a mother she was
The way she loved her boys
For them we pray to God.

She was a fighter
A believer too
Helped many people
Like me and you.

She believed in them
Gave them a chance
Gave them hope
And a second glance.

*When at last happiness,*
*She tried to find*
*The press were there*
*Showing the public eye.*

*This tragic life*
*Was suddenly ended*
*She died as she lived*
*With the press, in her face*
*We'll always remember her*
*As the goddess of the human race.*

*She is the queen of our hearts*
*The people's princess*
*We hope she'll find happiness*
*Now she's been laid to rest.*

*Diana, the Princess of Wales, can never be replaced.*

**Danni Turner**

## The Queen Of Hearts

*The Queen of Hearts*
*Went so many yards*
*To save the lives of so many*
*Now she has gone*
*Her love lives on*
*And shall remain in the hearts of so many.*

**Danielle Garster (10)**

### Dearest Diana,

*We're writing this little poem for you,*
*Because we feel so sad and blue.*
*Your caring, sharing, loving ways,*
*Your kindness, and your smiling gaze.*
*We will now and forever miss you so.*
*We'll never forget you, NEVER, NO!*
*Diana, the Princess, you played your part,*
*But to all of us, you are Queen of Hearts.*

*God bless you*
*Rest in peace.*

**Elaine, Chris, Elizabeth  (5)**
**& Andrew  (3)  Reeve**


### Diana

*Diana you are beautiful*
*Just like the stars in the sky*
*Even up in Heaven*
*You'll smile as the world goes by*

*You'll still pass down your feelings*
*So beautiful they were*
*Although you are up in Heaven*
*In our hearts*
*You are still here on earth.*

*Your two sons one day will be reunited*
*With your 'Dear Diana' in the sky,*
*Until then your work will achieve*
*So you 'Dear Diana' can rest in peace.*

**J Davis**

## Untitled

*Early on a Sunday morning,*
*My daughter phoned to say,*
*That Princess Di and Dodi,*
*Had been cruelly taken away.*

*The nation started crying,*
*'It's not true, it's all a lie,*
*Our Princess Di and Dodi,*
*Were too beautiful to die.'*

*When it finally started to sink in,*
*We thought of William and Harry,*
*What a terrible burden,*
*Their young shoulders had to carry.*

*Please, please cry, please shed a tear,*
*When you walk behind your mother,*
*She is the only one you'll have,*
*There will never be another.*

*They say in church you shed your tears,*
*And for that we are all glad,*
*The healing tears are what you need,*
*They'll help when you are sad.*

*Now sleep on dear Diana,*
*Your two boys will be fine,*
*Your family will make sure of that,*
*So now let PEACE BE THINE!*

**Margaret Jones**

## Princess Diana

*Everyone in the world is in shock and grief,*
*Her short life now seemed oh so brief,*
*She was unique, loved by everyone and adored,*
*The Queen of Hearts, happy and self assured,*
*There had been sadness and trouble in her life,*
*But she'd helped many others through illness*
*And strife,*
*Like a flame she shone bright,*
*To take her away is just not right,*
*She held out a hand to give a magic touch,*
*No words said, but the thought meant so much,*
*She was the world's most famous and adored*
*Princess,*
*At least her last weeks were full of happiness*
*And not distress,*
*She will never be forgotten, in our memories*
*She will stay,*
*Not just for now, tomorrow, but for every day,*
*God will now surely return the love that*
*She has given,*
*The cameras, flash bulbs, press have now*
*Been driven,*
*God will now welcome her with open arms,*
*Hold out his hands and take her palms,*
*You've done so much, and shown others the way,*
*Your good work will continue, we shall pray,*
*Your eternal flame will never go out,*
*Your love has not been wasted,*
*Of that there is no doubt,*
*So now Diana, rest in peace*
*As we must say goodbye,*
*Until one day we'll all meet again way up high,*
*Like a star in the sky, your light shines bright,*

*With wings spread on a journey through*
*Life's flight,*
*But nothing ever really ends,*
*Our thoughts, prayers and love to you we send.*

### Trudy Lapinskis

### Princess Diana

*Pomp and splendour all forgotten*
*Home they brought the sweet Princess,*
*Buried like a village maiden,*
*In the fields she loved the best.*
*Pure and beautiful they gave her*
*To a high and noble Prince,*
*And her simple faith sustained her*
*Till she died by sad mischance.*
*To her childhood home they brought her*
*Lord and Lady, Prince and Queen,*
*To the island where they laid her,*
*Low among the rushes green.*
*Where the willows cast their shadows,*
*Where the wild flowers bloom unseen,*
*There, no noisy throngs disturb her,*
*In a peaceful pastoral scene.*
*Then they laid her wreaths around her;*
*By the gentle breeze caressed,*
*Innocent of all emotion,*
*May her spirit there have rest.*

### Eirlys Hawkins Edwards

## To Diana

*Oh my Diana, snow white lily, rose of*
*heaven and earth.*
*Sweet spirit, sister of this lonely universe,*
*whose Empire is the name you wept upon.*
*In our heart's memory we suspend to thee these votive wreaths of*
*beautiful memories.*

*Poor captive bird, who from thy narrow cage,*
*poured out such love and kindness that might have assuaged the*
*rugged hearts that imprisoned you.*
*We're not deaf to all your rightful yearnings,*
*through their own cold powers, to speak*
*in feeble warnings.*

*This shall be my rose and poem to thee.*
*Whose petals by my tears are dead indeed.*
*But soft and fragrant is the blossom,*
*Oh my princess it has to thorn to wound thy bosom,*
*because you have beheld the form of love.*

*With unrelaxing speed the whole world heard*
*of your death,*
*with vision and love they have cried aloud,*
*sleep or death shall not divide us long,*
*we know the cause of your departure,*
*our love for you is far too strong.*

*Oh dream of youth, oh breath of heaven,*
*it is a woe too deep for tears.*
*Which night and time have quenched for ever,*
*Oh death's white and winged steed took away*
*our flower and trampled down the weed.*

*Goodbye our princess of the people,*
*may you be forever in God's arms sleeping,*
*both our birthdays are written in the sky*
*we were both born years apart,*
*the first day of July, we will be linked together*
*until I will die.*

**Elizabeth Clancy**

## Princess Diana, The People's Princess

*You were a light burning so bright,*
*Now it has gone,*
*But you are still here,*
*In our hearts forever strong.*

*Your kind smiling face,*
*And your warm loving touch,*
*Is what the world remembers,*
*We will all miss you so much.*

*You had heartache and pain through the years,*
*But now you will shed no more tears,*
*At last you found happiness with the man that*
*you love,*
*Only now it is eternal in the Heavens above.*

*Your loss to the world is so sad, we will be*
*Thinking of you now and forever,*
*You are in our hearts always and forever.*

**C D Gaywood**

## Diana, The Brave

Not in cold stone, nor slabs of wood,
For neither could capture that which was good,
No sculpture could render the essence we craved
Our hearts must remember, Diana, the Brave.

Friend to the lost, in a world full of greed,
A symbol of hope to those most in need,
Think of the homeless, the hungry, the victims
                        she saved,
The poor shall remember, Diana the Brave.

Still now sad hearts, for she is at rest,
Her work here is done, a work that was blessed,
A touch of her hand was all that she gave,
The sick shall remember, Diana, the Brave.

Not in cold stone, or Memorial Park,
To remember the beautiful, Queen of our Hearts,
Remember her light, in a world that was grey,
We will never forget you, Diana, the Brave.

**Mike Smith**

## Diana

D  is for devoted, to everything she did.
I  is for irreplaceable, to a world in which she lived.
A  is for angel, looking down from the sky.
N  is for never, having to say goodbye.
A  is for answers, why did she have to die.

**Paula Ringer**

## Diana, Princess Of The World's People

*A tender touch, a friendly smile,*
*Was always to be your style,*

*Many pathways stretched before you,*
*For you did choose the very one to*

*Our hearts, and in our minds we*
*Knew you loved us so naturally and free,*

*Then suddenly you were not there for us,*
*We were broken-hearted every one of us,*

*Flowers were all we had to show the heavens,*
*The tears as raindrops fell to floods and ravines*

*Which flowed to a sea of love,*
*To set free the brightest dove*

*Of peace and goodness ever imagined on earth,*
*By mere mortals living around the breadth and girth*

*Of our Mother Earth.*

**Bruce Allen**


## Diana

*Words are oh so many.*
*Deeds are oh so few.*
*Diana carried hers out.*
*Have I, has the world, have you?*

**Brenda Kelly**

## The People's Champion

A silent witness I look on,
Along with a nation, your passing I mourn;
For the world is now a much emptier place,
Without you, our Princess, to embrace.
How could it be, that one so pure of heart,
At such a young age, should have to part.
The people's champion you became,
You helped to alleviate so much pain.
You became a victim of your deeds,
Not one of selfishness or of greed;
But of giving and sharing, loving and caring,
Never aloof or condescending.
From AIDS to Palsy to the evil landmine,
You unselfishly gave, your precious time.
A few kind words, a gentle touch,
To those who were suffering, this meant so much.
Never giving a thought for yourself,
Into others' problems you would deeply delve.
When you held the dying in your arms,
For your own safety, you had no qualms;
The love you showed was pure and true,
A gift you gave to many, not just a few.
Never did you ask, for anything in return,
The respect of the world, you did not demand
                              but earn.

The media brought you into our lives,
You were always there with us, morning and night.
An Ambassador last, a mother first,
In public or private, your life was cursed.
You became so popular, with your deeds so great,
That your very being, was to seal your fate.

*The paparazzi invaded your life,*
*As if they had, some God-given right;*
*Not for one moment, were you left alone,*
*Whether holidaying abroad, or with your*
                                        *children at home.*

*But now you have eternal peace,*
*The kind before, you found only in sleep.*
*We will never forget you, though you have gone,*
*Your words and your deeds, will forever live on;*
*For we shall always have, our memories and dreams,*
*Of a fairy tale Princess, who in our hearts, will*
                                        *'always be Queen'.*

### Peter Redpath

### Diana

*If there's a heaven up above,*
*Look after our princess, whom we love.*
*I'll never forget when you were lying in your bed,*
*And I came in and told you, 'DIANA WAS DEAD.'*
*Those greedy photographers we'll never forgive,*
*For Diana is gone, and they live on.*

*And to your tender loving sons,*
*We'll never forget them Wills and Harry, who*
*One day will marry, you too will love*
*Your children, like your mum did with you,*
*You too, like your mum will be such fun,*
*Keeping her special, ever burning. loving flame alive,*
*In you, and your children's children forever.*

*God bless you sweet princess.*

### R J and M E Boyd

## Farewell Beloved Princess

It was in her eyes, in her eyes,
A multitude of grief and sighs.
Married in hope and early betrayal,
Forsaken, hurting and so dismayed,
Searching in agony of grief,
Oh how to find some light relief.
A broken and compassionate heart,
Such a longing to play her part
For the lame and lost for whom she cared,
And all their miseries she shared.
But set aside, yes set aside
By one she loved and how she cried.
She cried with tears that could not flow
And on and on she had to go -
Functions, visits, opening fetes,
Crowded diaries with duty dates,
Seeking, seeking how to stop hurting
Whilst all around the press were skirting.
But, dear reader, don't blame the press,
Backtrack to what began this mess,
Go back to the very beginning
She more sinned against than sinning.
Royal protection suddenly lost,
Another's sin to pay the cost,
All she hoped for now quite frail
And not allowed to weep or wail.
The need now to defend herself
With loss of stature, threatened health.
Lovely Diana now at peace,
Now your agonies will cease.
With Our Lord's mercy and His grace
You will be in a better place.

*Woe to the Church which kept silent on sin*
*Responsible for the state you were in.*
*What can be said in honour of thee?*
*The axe must be laid to the root of the tree*
*To convict of such hypocrisy.*

**Pearl Kumar**

## Diana

*You came into our lives like a breath of fresh air,*
*The brightest star in a cloudless night sky,*
*So young and  innocent,*
*A fairytale princess with a Prince Charming.*
*We thought you would be our queen.*
*Loved by millions from all over the world.*
*Wherever you travelled you touched people's hearts,*
*Touching, kissing, hugging the young, old*
*and sick,*
*Caring came so naturally.*
*You live on through two boys, whom you so*
*deeply loved,*
*In their laughter, their smiles, their tears and*
*their hearts.*
*No one can hurt you now Diana, as God's angels*
*watch over you.*
*So don't be lonely, we will never forget,*
*Our princess, we once thought would be queen.*

**J L Fielding**

## Princess Diana

*Words are not enough to express how I feel,*
*it's hard to believe you are not here,*
*you touched so many hearts*
*with a kind word and a smile,*
*You brought sunshine into our lives,*
*and gave us hope*
*when we gave up caring,*
*Your sons are so beautiful*
*just like you*
*I myself know what they are going through*
*You brought them up in such a way*
*that they remind us of you*
*with each passing day.*
*Now our country has lost a princess*
*and Heaven has gained the most*
*beautiful queen.*
*Our 'Queen of Hearts'.*

**Samantha White**


## Diana

*She came like a flower in summer*
*blossoming, shining so bright,*
*Her petals soft and warm*
*still brightly shone at night.*

*But this flower has lost its petals*
*but not in vain it's known*
*Each one touched by her softness*
*in love and companion has grown.*

**Julie McKenzie**

## Goodbye England's Rose

*You touched the hearts of many people*
*Across the world your love you shared*
*You brought the nation close together*
*To let the people know you cared*

*For all you cared for, all the help you gave*
*We could see you were born a fighter*
*We have watched, listened and learned from you*
*We now see that our future is brighter*

*With you beside us we would never give up*
*For you would guide us through the hard parts*
*When days were tough you would keep us strong*
*You are our Queen of Hearts*

*In person we thank you for all your support*
*What you gave was a comforting manner*
*For charities, illnesses and lives torn apart*
*God sent an angel and called her Diana*

*Although with our eyes we cannot see you*
*The love in our heart still grows*
*The angels do call and you must go*
*With love, goodbye England's rose*

*In loving memory of Diana, Princess of Wales*

**Steven Tanner**

## Untitled

*You were a special princess*
*There will never be another*
*A princess who was so very kind*
*And a loving mother.*

*You warmed the hearts of everyone*
*When you were very daring*
*Walking through those minefields*
*It showed you were so caring.*

*You have worked wonders in this world*
*That others could not do*
*You have helped thousands of people*
*They owe their thanks to you.*

*A princess of understanding*
*Always nimble on your toes*
*A lovely pretty princess*
*A lovely 'English Rose'.*

*But now you're up in Heaven*
*Looking down on all of us*
*You might be saying to yourself*
*What is all the fuss?*

*So rest in peace my angel*
*We are very sad*
*But I know you are so happy*
*Up there with your Dad.*

**R W Cox**

### Princess Diana

The news came out you passed away
The disbelief continued throughout the day.
Pictures of you flooded the world.
Carpets of flowers spread far and wide
With words of sorrow that you had died.
Your care and compassion went through
the people's hearts.
You graced the world with your
charm and beauty.
Time stood still for a while,
Then songs of praise rang out aloud.
The memories of you will linger on
as night to day for evermore.
The people came from far and wide
to watch you go where the stars shine.

### Dot Langan


### For Diana Princess Of Wales

From a stark underpass in Paris,
With the first chill thrust of dawn,
Came the news of the death
Of a beautiful Princess,
Who held the wide world in thrall.

Diana of the loving heart,
May you be given peace.
And may love like yours,
So freely given,
Evermore increase.

### Ron Delacruz

## Diana, Princess Of Love

D  evotion you showed to sick children you met,
   You were and always will be the 'People's
   Princess'.

I  ntuition to know the troubles and strife
   That ordinary people have suffered through
   life.

A  ttention kindness love and caring
   The 'Queen of Hearts' was never sparing.

N  atural compassion for the weak young and old.
   The irreplaceable beautiful English rose.

A  ngels came down from Heaven above.
   They took you away the nation's
   'Princess of Love'.

**Christine Robinson**


## Diana

You were an Angel, sent down from God above
To bestow upon the world, the gift of perfect love
Healing hands, the sick you did touch
The homeless, the needy, you cared so much
Constantly campaigning, to make us all aware
Of the plight, of those injured by landmines . . .
                              Hidden where?
Tragically taken, your death will not be in vain
The World laments, Heaven's gain
Crystal tears, as the Nation weeps
At the loss of our Princess, so Perfect, so Dear.

**Susan L Metcalfe**

## Dearest Diana

To say you're missed, is an understatement
It tears us apart inside
We flush a range of feelings
The tears we cannot hide.

The pain grows within us
The anger it does show
The nation is shocked and grieving
We don't want to let you go.

You left the earth so quickly
We never did say goodbye
Your death was masked with tragedy
And all we do is cry.

The people's princess, the Queen of Hearts
Is what they are calling you
I for one must agree
After seeing all the things you'd do.

You were always someone special
And never a thought away
I'll remember you forever
And hold you dear each day.

**Helen Pearce**

## Diana

*You were in the news almost
every day,
Giving a constant fashion
display,
Your superb figure was second
to none,
And before you died you were
having fun,
Visiting places far and wide,
With Dodi Fayed by your
side,
Travelling the world by boat
and jet,
Mixing with the upper set,
What else could we expect
from you?
You looked a dream and
reigned supreme,
Wherever you went the newsmen
flocked,
To photograph your latest
frock,
Now you've gone, the world's
in shock,
Our beloved princess,
Britain's Rock,
We will never forget you,
our beautiful Di,
You're the brightest star, in
the sky*

**Lucy Scholey**

## 'Diana', A Princess Loved

*The flame of life erased, Diana you have gone,*
*To your final resting place, but your memory will live on,*
*Your beauty and grace, are world-renowned,*
*Both to the rich, and to the poor,*
*Your fight for the homeless, also Leprosy*
*and more,*
*All people world-wide love you,*
*Some though, you've never even met,*
*Others know Diana, your love they shan't forget,*
*AIDS sufferers everywhere, know they too have your love,*
*A love which is now in Heaven, with the Lord above,*
*For little children everywhere, Diana*
*you're a star,*
*Up in the blue, blue Heaven, shining from afar,*
*A waste of life, still filled with love,*
*A love which will last for evermore,*
*You fight for the landmines, is one*
*we can't ignore,*
*Diana, lovely Diana, now Heaven is your home,*
*I hope you find true happiness*
*Through this very sad release*
*Our 'Princess of the People',*
*Diana 'rest in peace'.*

**John Webb**

## Queen Of Our Hearts

We know she's up in heaven
Watching, looking down
And God was there to meet her
To present her with her crown
And there she is an angel
Just like she was before
God was so impatient
To get her to his door.

Diana Queen of Hearts
How dearly we'll miss you
You left us here behind
Where folk like you are few
The world has lost its only queen
A mother to us all
When you had to leave us
That shining star did fall.

But you'll never be forgotten
The joy to hearts you brought
You'll always remain with us
In every single thought
The world will be a sadder place
Now that you have left.
To take you away from us
Was God's greatest theft.

But God took you up into His house
And angel now you'll be
You shone your light way up high
For all of us to see.

*So Diana Queen of Hearts*
*This poem I wrote for you*
*Just to let you know*
*How dearly we'll miss you.*

*With my deepest sympathy.*

**Patrick Hennessy**


## Princess Diana

*Your life had spells of sadness,*
*And yet you gave so much,*
*You had so much compassion*
*For the people whom you touched.*

*You stretched your hand*
*Out to them all.*
*The lepers and the ones with AIDS,*
*The love you felt was on your face*
*When little babies you embraced.*

*You've left behind two fine young boys*
*Who will be lost without their Mum,*
*But they will be so very proud*
*Of all the good things you have done.*

*We never will forget the care*
*You showed to people everywhere,*
*The light you shone is shining still*
*Within our hearts,*
*And always will.*

**Mary Rule**

## A Human Angel

This world will be a sadder place,
Without her beautiful, smiling face,
Those eyes so blue and hair so fair,
She showed this world, her love and care.

She gave comfort to the sick and dying,
With a shy smile and inside quietly crying,
Offering up a silent prayer,
Hoping that someone would always be there.

To her sons, she was a caring mother,
Her love for them was like no other,
She has left them a gift, a legacy,
Of love, humbleness and serenity.

She will be remembered in the coming years,
Not with sadness or with tears,
But with love, for playing her part,
A human Angel, a 'Queen of Hearts'.

**Patricia White**


## A Poem For A Princess And Her Love

Diana you came to us
from a star in heaven
and now you have returned
to re-kindle a star with Dodi
shining upon us like a magic light
Burning brighter each night
together forever to show
us the light.

**S Corrigan**

## Princess Of Love

*A little star from up above*
*Fell on her head, for us to love*
*The little star was for Princess Di,*
*She touched our hearts*
*And caught our eye.*

*For us there could, be no other*
*A beautiful Princess*
*A loving Mother.*

*We shed our tears*
*She was the best*
*At Althorp House*
*She's laid to rest.*

*We will always, remember our Princess Di*
*When we're alone, we will sit and cry.*
*No-one else could take her place*
*For what she did, for the human race*
*We love her now, although she's gone*

*Goodbye Diana,*
> *Our Beautiful One.*

**Abbey Flack**

## Diana

*They say the good die young,*
*    and sadly this is true.*
*But to take you so suddenly*
*    when you still had so much to give and do.*
*You gave the frail and weak the will to live*
*    to the injured you gave hope*
*If not just by your presence*
*    it would be with a laugh or joke.*
*You are in all our hearts*
*    and you brightened all our days*
*You changed so many people's lives*
*    in oh so many ways.*
*You were an angel loaned by God*
*    to teach us to care and love.*
*Now God has taken back His angel*
*    to watch us from above.*
*Let's hope we've learned your lessons well*
*    and your life has not all been in vain*
*That we bring love and joy into the world*
*    and not the grief and pain.*
*You were the 'People's Princess'*
*    a truly special English Rose*
*A star that nestles in the heavens*
*    that everybody knows.*

**Wendy Cooper**

## Untitled

*Still we mourn, still we grieve,*
*That our beloved Princess had to leave,*
*Who will bring joy, hope and love?*
*Our Diana will, from Heaven above.*

*We all lost a Princess, the boys lost their*
*Mum,*
*But we will carry out her wishes in the*
*years to come.*

*We are richer for knowing our Queen*
*amongst Queens,*
*Be happy Diana on your*
            *ISLAND OF DREAMS.*

### Annette Steele


## A Poem For Diana

*We, the unknown, who are lucky*
*We, the unknown, who are plain*
*We live our lives in obscurity*
*But no one knows the pain*

*But you, who were so public*
*You, who were not plain*
*Lived in a constant spotlight*
*And everyone knew your pain*

*I pray you now are tranquil*
*I pray your sons feel the same*
*Safe in the arms of God's love*
*The world will not be the same.*

### Lorna Sim

## Queen Of Hearts

*(This poem was inspired by the wave of love for Diana, Princess of Wales, after her sudden death,*
*31st August 1997)*

*She wanted to be called the Queen of Hearts*
*And won a deep devotion giv'n to few.*
*Her warmth, compassion and her ringing laugh*
*Attracted love and admiration too.*

*'I was in prison and you came to Me.'*
*'When I was hungry, then you gave Me meat.'*
*'Do this for others and it is for Me.'*
*He spoke and her obedience was complete.*

*Diana, Princess, mingled with the crowds,*
*Picked up the children, touched the troubled soul.*
*She comforted, relieved their suffering,*
*And those who met her felt they were made whole.*

*She loved the poor, the outcast, the distressed.*
*She visited the prisoners and the ill.*
*She followed Our Lord's teaching and she tried*
*In all her ways to do His Holy Will.*

*A light is out; extinguished is a flame.*
*Who will continue all the work begun?*
*She cared so much that landmines should*
                                    *be banned,*
*The world a better place to raise her son.*

*The silent mourners watched as the hearse passed*
*And tossed their flowers - tokens of their love.*
*Diana left this earth a poorer place*
*And went to her eternal home above.*

**Joyce M Turner**

## Diana

*Four happy people in a car,*
*Travelling through a tunnel.*
*Suddenly excited bikers*
*Either side, thrusting papers*
*At the passengers, and driver,*
*Thoughtless, shouting, blocking sight*
*Of the bollards and narrow space.*
*Suddenly the car swung right*
*Speeding to avoid the bikers*
*Struck hard at a central bollard.*
*Only one survived.*

*Oceans of flowers*
*Brightening walls, grey roads*
*But not the sad hearts*
*Of people mourning*
*A Princess, beautiful,*
*Hardworking, kind, helpful*
*To all, irrespective*
*Of colour, race, gender,*
*Crashed with friends*
*Speeding through a tunnel,*
*To England.*

**M K Wickrema**

## Diana Of The Lake

*On your lonely green island in the lake*
*you sleep in peace.*
*The sun will shine, the little waves break*
*when the wind sighs.*

*Birdsong at morning, moonlight at night*
*the patter of rain,*
*but your bright enthusiasm, your golden light*
*will never shine again.*

*You lit a flame that will forever burn,*
*we must never forget*
*your care for the sick, the deprived, and learn*
*to follow your dream*

*So, goodbye 'Diana of the Lake'*
*Rest in peace.*

**Marge Chamberlain**


## Diana, A Vision Of Pure Perfection

*The magic of a princess*
*is just so hard to find*
*That when you look at Diana*
*You come to realise why.*

*Gaze into her loving eyes*
*Past the radiant complexion*
*You then see why she was chosen.*

*'A vision of pure perfection'.*

**Rachel Whitford (14)**

## Queen Of Our Hearts

*Diana, Princess of Wales*
*Queen of Hearts throughout the world*
*A beautiful lady who cared for others*
*She was also a loving and caring mother*
*Her life was a mixture of ups and downs*
*We have seen her smiles, also her frowns*
*She was more than a princess, that we could see*
*She was a nice human being, just like you and me*
*Unique and wonderful, charming and true*
*Not only a Princess of Beauty outside*
*But on the inside too.*
*Hew new relationship with Dodi Fayed*
*Made her happy and content*
*From her smile you could tell.*
*What happened today was a real tragedy*
*To lose her young life in such a way.*
*It has broken the hearts of all, I can say*
*All over the world the people will mourn*
*The loss of a princess with a heart of gold.*
*A princess whose smiling and caring ways*
*Will have her remembered for many a day*
*Diana, the Princess, the 'Queen of our Hearts'*
*She will be remembered for all she has done*
*By all of the people whose hearts she has won.*
*Rest in peace, Diana, our 'Beautiful Princess'.*

**Christine Stirling**

## The Colours Of Diana

*So young you appeared in blue on his arm,*
*The sapphire and diamonds mirrored your charm.*
*So sweet and naive we held you close that year,*
*As you emerged from St Paul's we all*
*raised a cheer.*
*Your work took you tirelessly from home*
*to abroad,*
*The sun would shine and the rain it poured.*
*Your visits so special to everyone there,*
*Each patient knew: here was someone to care.*
*You brought with you sunshine, like a beacon*
*of light*
*Into people's hearts, you shone so bright.*
*You dazzled us, glittering, shining like a star,*
*Your gowns in New York told of who you are.*
*A sparkle of hope you gave to the dying,*
*Their spirits lifted to know you were trying*
*To brighten their day, to make them feel good,*
*You gave so much love in any way you could.*
*Dressed in red, your head held high,*
*Now happier in life, no longer shy.*
*You always carried flowers, you are an*
*eternal rose*
*Whose beauty will live on in us, as your days come to a close.*
*Your life is spread before us now, a sea of dazzling hue,*
*If only you could see that all our love still shines for you.*
*A nation in black mourns you like no other,*
*Not only to your boys but to us you were*
*a mother,*
*Embracing us no matter what, when others feared to touch,*
*We want to tell you now how you meant so*
*very much.*

*A life with so much left to live, so tragically*
*cut short,*
*We know that in your final hour, the bravest ones they fought*
*To save you, to restore your energy and zest,*
*But now in death we hope you will be allowed*
*to rest.*

### Avril Reay

## Diana

*The world's greatest Star*
*You helped all of those around you*
*No matter how near or far*
*The help you gave to those in need*
*Shone out like a sparkling star*
*You brightened the lives of others*
*Their faces shone so bright*
*Even through a dreary day*
*They brightened up at night*
*I am sure your work will be continued*
*After this our saddest day*
*With William and Harry we are with*
*Them all the way*
*You will never be forgotten*
*In this country and afar*
*God bless you forever,*
       *Diana, our brightest Star.*

### George Moneypenny

## Diana, Princess Of Wales

*Our greatest sleeping beauty*
*has left the world alone,*
*who will look after us now Lord?*
*Who will give the poor a home?*
*She brought us peace and strengthened us*
*and made us realise that it's true,*
*So let's help William and Harry*
*to let them make it through.*

*She shone a light from her heart*
*and cared for everyone,*
*But the very sad thing about it*
*is that she died so very young.*

*So please be silent for just a minute*
*to think about her tragic end,*
*So just think about it*
*this is the only thing*
*that she can't mend!*

**Katherine Jenkins  (11)**

## An Ode To A Rose

*To our darling Diana*
*The Princess of Wales*
*Who blossomed into the most*
*beautiful rose,*
*I will never forget your smiling face,*
*or the two buds you left behind to*
*blossom and bloom in your place.*

**D Wickens**

## To Those Who Loved Diana Look Upon Your Wall

*Look upon her portrait, that*
*Hangs upon your wall,*
*Feel the love and passion,*
*That rests within her soul;*
*You placed your love and honour,*
*Upon this lovely maiden,*
*So elegant and graceful,*
*So courtly and so tall:*

*She's forever in your memory,*
*The love endowed upon her;*
*You gave to her your all.*
*She's no longer with you,*
*Except within your soul;*
*Hold onto your lovely dreams;*
*Never let her go;*
*Your dreams are for eternity;*
*Our angels told us so.*

**George Ponting**


## A Poem For the People's Princess

*The Journey of Life cut painfully short*
*The Sorrow we feel for the Love that she sought*
*Love and Compassion the gifts that she brought*
*Now just Contemplation and silent thoughts.*

**R J Oldroyd**

## Jewel In The Crown

*You truly were our only jewel in the crown*
*Now we have only tears in which we'll*
*surely drown*
*Where before we had your beautiful smiling face*
*Now you are gone, in our hearts there's an*
*empty space*
*A wonderful shining gem you were to the nation*
*Full of love and compassion, a most*
*unique creation*
*And when you wore your heart on your sleeve*
*In your honesty we could always believe*

*When we heard of your most untimely calling*
*The whole Nation's tears started falling*
*We will always remember all the good things*
*you did*
*But now lovely Princess a peaceful rest to you*
*we bid.*

### Lesley J Line

## Wind-Blown Petals

*The permanence of plastic blooms*
*would not express so much*
*as wind-blown petals left to bless*
*a dead princess's touch.*

### Barbara Smoker

## So, So Sad

D on't know this feeling, it's awful strange, see
I cannot explain what is happening to me,
A ppetite half gone, deep thoughts, devotion,
N o real words to describe my emotion,
A lways thought grief was for friends and family,

P atriotism maybe, but I suppose that depends,
R ight now I feel as if I've lost a sister,
I s this correct? No ! But somehow I shall miss her,
N ewspaper portraits of glistening eyes bright,
C ar headlights beaming right through the night,
E ssences of freshness, hope and charity you brought,
S olitude and loneliness, the establishment you
    fought,
S crutiny and sorrow, sometimes made you forlorn,

O f course, we won't know how much, your heart
    was torn,
F or me it seemed, all that changed the day you
    fell in love,

W ith Dodi Al Fayed, maybe an angel from above,
A nd all good things come to an end, but not before
    it starts!
L eaving us the way you did pierces so many hearts,
E ternity is so, so sad you'll never 'ever, ever'
    be replaced,
S orely missed, always loved, you 'made a difference'
    in this space.

*Goodnight, sleep tight*

## Mike

## Diana Princess of Wales . . .

*How perfect the grace*
*That wondrous smile*
*How lovely the face*
*That encaptured rank and file*
*With poise and perception*
*Warmth with no exception*
*Nothing too great*
*Nothing too small*
*You entered the scene*
*Answering the call*
*With comfort and care*
*And a sensuous air*
*To ease pain and distress*
*Our loving, caring, beautiful Princess . . .*

*Now gone from our lives, to be a shining star*
*We will look to the night sky, to where you are*
*Your memory will not fade, for what you achieved*
*For we will remember the day,*
              *when the nation grieved . . .*

## John Franks

## Farewell Diana

*Farewell Diana - Princess of Wales*
*You will be sadly missed in the towns and the vales*
*Beautiful princess no longer doing good in the land*
*Walks with God now, hand in hand.*

*It is such a shame you will never have known*
*The love for you that has been shown*
*Candles lit and flowers laid*
*A kind tribute the people paid.*

*We love and miss you is the message in the card*
*We cannot believe you're gone*
*The world will seem a darker place*
*Without the light that shone.*

**Anita Wonnacott**

## Diana

| | |
|---|---|
| *The nation lost its* | *Daughter* |
| *the day that we lost you* | |
| *the country recoiled in horror* | |
| *couldn't believe it was true* | |
| *At first you were* | *Insecure* |
| *not sure how to play your part* | |
| *but soon you came to realise* | |
| *you had power to touch our heart* | |
| *Happiness when your children* | *Arrived* |
| *and you had so much love* | |
| *I'm sure you are watching them* | |
| *from your seat above* | |
| *Your life was too short* | *No doubt* |
| *and we were all so sad* | |
| *but when we think of all your good* | |
| *it makes our heart feel glad* | |
| *We thought you were an* | *Angel* |
| *and to your people you're no less* | |
| *always you'll be remembered* | |
| *as DIANA, the 'People's Princess'.* | |

**Joy Benford**

## Diana

*Beauty, an aura a golden glow*
*Emanating, dazzling all who saw,*
*Compassion from the depths of her heart*
*flowed out,*
*To touch every soul that she happened to meet.*

*A privilege and honour, they all agreed,*
*From the dignitaries, workers down to waifs in*
*the street,*
*She treated them all to kindness and grace.*
*Faith, love and sorrow mirroring o'er her face.*

*She gave her all to the ones most in need,*
*The sick and the dying, the maimed - any creed,*
*Her presence warmth and caring enough for*
*them all*
*Their troubles and problems she showed to*
*the world.*

*She proved to us all that we should not have fear*
*Of sickness and death, that we should draw near,*
*To those who are suffering, to help where we can,*
*No matter what age or what colour the hand.*

*They'll never forget her, throughout the world,*
*Her image portrayed holding aged and child,*
*Soothing the suff'ring wherever she could,*
*With kind words and gestures,*
*but most of all Love.*

**Margaret J H Goudie**

## Diana - Princess Of The People

When I heard the news that Sunday morn
I felt so sad and all forlorn
I tried to go about my daily chores
But felt the light blocked through closed doors.

Diana Royal, Princess of Wales
Smile and beauty by all was hailed
Your love and compassion for the common man
I'm sure was all part of God's special plan.

The way you cradled those tiny mites
Because you were touched by their plights
These acts came from your very soul
Knowing for them life had taken its toll.

You gave your princess a wonderful start
Love and devotion straight from your heart
Your memory they will always treasure
Missing you always, forgetting you never.

Dear Angel of Mercy take your rest
For on this earth you stood the test
A shining example to all walks of life
At last free from sorrow and all strife.

**S Bradshaw**

## Queen In Our Hearts

*A lovely Princess inside and out*
*A friend to everyone without a doubt*
*A beautiful smile, a shake of the hand*
*Your magic spread all over the land*
*You'll always be Queen in our hearts*

*A direction you had, with so much to achieve*
*We do feel lost and so many will grieve*
*Your spirit will live, I'm sure in us all*
*We'll think of England's Rose and stands*
*proud and tall*
*You'll always be queen in our hearts*

*Now you are free from torment and pain*
*Free as a Dove and at peace once again*
*We'll have peace in our hearts and do*
*as you wished*
*Oh England's Rose you'll be sadly missed.*

**Kathy Dring**


## Diana

*Diana was the queen of our heart,*
*And now our world's been blown apart,*
*A massive void never to be filled,*
*Was caused the day Diana was killed.*

*She was an angel from above,*
*Who gave everyone the same kind of love,*
*She didn't care what people said,*
*She cared about AIDS and landmines instead.*

She wasn't perfect, but then who is,
But performed her duties with bubble and fizz,
She loved all the people whatever their ills,
But mainly her love was for Harry and Wills.

Her cheeky grin, her beautiful face,
The world will be a worse off place,
You'll be remembered till the world does cease,
Diana, I hope you can now rest in peace.

**Kevin Rounce**

## A Sonnet To Princess Diana

You're the Princess of Hearts, body and mind,
You will be remembered, forever, by all mankind,
All with whom you worked and gave time will
                                    miss your vision,
Who could take your place and continue
                                    your mission,
You were outstanding, with a beauty fair,
And set the trends in fashion and hair,
In your awe, people would freeze,
Oh! Diana, you knew how to put them at ease,
Your life, was, so tragically taken,
The whole wide world, so totally shaken,
So why do the good have to die young?
When your life had only just begun,
But in our hearts and minds your memory prevails
Diana, Princess of Wales.

**Leon Hubbard**

## Diana - Gone But Not Forgotten

*No ceremonies to perform,*
*Just remember her as she was born,*
*For the things she did the best,*
*And to disregard the rest.*

*There's no time to give in,*
*Although this time, sorrow brings,*
*Remember the happy days,*
*And keep her love always.*

*No tears, for she has gone,*
*But remember all she's done,*
*And keep her good works going,*
*And the care and love flowing.*

*To hold each happy moment,*
*And all the time we spent,*
*Living our lives together,*
*For the love will last forever.*

**Bruce Ripley**


## Thoughts For William And Harry

*I thought of you both this morning*
*as I have done all this week,*
*I imagine how you're feeling*
*as you struggle with your grief.*

*Just remember all the good times*
*and all the fun you had.*
*The fairground rides, McDonald's*
*sunshine hols and all those hugs.*

*Your mother loved you so much*
*by your side she will always stay,*
*her arms will never leave you*
*as you travel along life's way.*

*A million thoughts are with you*
*from a nation who really cares.*
*Your loving and compassionate Mum*
*will live in our hearts for years.*

**Margaret Gillson**

### Goodbye, England's Rose

*To a beloved Princess*
*Who rose way, way above the rest*
*A heart so loving and with tender care*
*Brought precious moments for one and all to share*
*Your work is done,*
*You did your best,*
*Now you've gone to have a rest.*
*We loved you then,*
*We love you still*
*So take our hearts on this last journey,*
*I know you will*
*To live with God*
*Who picked you to be the best.*
*Goodnight, God Bless*
*Dear Princess.*

**D C J Jones**

## A Tribute To Diana

*She's gone from amongst us*
*A bright shining star*
*Diana the Princess*
*We adored from afar*
*Her short life has ended in sorrow and pain*
*To me she would have been a beautiful queen*
*Her two little boys she loved and adored*
*A loving mum sadly no more.*
*All children she loved with a love sincere*
*No matter what colour race or creed.*
*So I wish I could wake from this horrible dream*
*But I am not dreaming it's all so real*
*Our beautiful Diana we'll see no more.*

## Margaret Walker

## The English Rose

*To Diana, our very own English Rose,*
*A Lady of beauty and dignified pose,*
*So caring and gentle, and so full of fun,*
*Admired and loved by everyone,*
*But Diana's not gone, she is just sleeping.*
*She wouldn't expect us all to be weeping.*
*If you look to the sky, you will see a star,*
*It's our Diana, looking down from afar.*
*She was a Princess with a heart of gold.*
*She cared for the sick, the young and the old,*
*She cared for the needy and those full of stress*
*So sleep gentle Princess,*
*Goodnight and God Bless.*

## T Woods

## Lovely Diana

*Our lovely Diana*
*Queen of the sky*
*Why oh why! Did you have to die?* ·
*So many hearts broken in two*
*You know we thought the world of you*
*Did the children need a new nurse?*
*Someone to care when they got hurt?*
*Did you hold them in your loving arms?*
*Did they succumb to your many charms?*
*Let's keep alive her memory*
*This treasure we won't forget*
*Her special way with children*
*Will be with us a long time yet.*

**Rachel Cresswell**


## That Fateful Day

*(Written on the morning of the sad demise of Diana, Princess of Wales)*

*The thirty-first of August*
*Year nineteen ninety seven*
*The day our lovely princess died*
*And God welcomed her to Heaven*

*All lights on earth went out that day*
*But the stars shone bright above*
*As angels greeted her with joy*
*We mourned our own lost love.*

**Gwynn Watt**

## Lost

*Your passing has taught this world a lesson,*
*Your life has taught this world to care,*
*Your love has taught this world emotion,*
*At Heaven I stand and stare.*

*Your beauty was there for all to see,*
*Your eyes they shone so bright,*
*Right now the world has stopped to see,*
*Our Princess is out of sight.*

*In life you were the victim,*
*In death the people's Queen,*
*In Heaven you can look down and see,*
*In life, what you had never seen.*

*Yesterday you were the Queen of Hearts,*
*But peace you were not given,*
*Today the world cries oceans,*
*As our Queen finds peace in Heaven.*

*Although you're gone, you're still around,*
*Memories so clear to see,*
*Thank God that they will never hound,*
*His favourite child who tried to flee.*

*The light has tragically disappeared,*
*The world in disbelief,*
*I hope you find what you had sought*
*As this world sits numb in grief.*

*Everyone you touched in life,*
*The tears, the loss, the scream,*
*Is this really happening?*
*They hope it's all a dream.*

*Your sons and family in our thoughts,*
*The pain they feel, we do,*
*Together we unite in sorrow,*
*For the one who was one of few.*

*Diana, Diana, you'll never die,*
*Your love is in the air,*
*Alive forever in our hearts,*
*Now your love this world can share.*

**Melville Campbell**


## *Goodnight Sweet Princess!*

*Words cannot express how sad the nation feels today,*
*You will always be remembered for your kind and*
*loving ways.*
*You put a smile on so many faces,*
*Visiting the sick and needy in so many places,*
*Just as you found happiness your life ends on earth,*
*but in heaven you and Dodi will re-birth,*
*You brought joy to everyone especially your two*
*Lovely sons, who today are so proud to have you as*
*their Mum,*
*'Cause to everyone you are the number one.*
*No-one can replace our beautiful princess, who's*
*happy in heaven, now safe and at rest.*
*No-one ever will forget the special person you are,*
*you were a princess, a saint, now an angel at last.*

*Goodnight sweet Princess.*

**Jenny Coyle (17)**

## Diana Princess Of Wales

*Another star shines in the Heavens tonight*
*Why oh why? People cry in the night*
*Of sorrow and pain she had her share*
*A person who shone was England's crown*
*She was sad and happy and always chained*
*A smile so bright and then a frown,*
*She wanted freedom to love not be restrained*
*The world loved her through her tears and stress*
*They wanted her to have happiness*
*She has left a void too deep to fill*
*Her eyes are closed her heart is still*
*Her hopes her dreams will never be*
*Her boys growing up she will never see*
*But on her last journey of tear-filled miles*
*People will always remember her brilliant smiles.*

## J Straker

## Farewell To Our Princess

*A bright light has gone out in the world,*
*Flowers came from everywhere, grieving all around,*
*People in their millions brought the country to a stop,*
*Silence was golden, you could hear a pin drop,*
*They lined the route to say farewell,*
*To take our princess home,*
*Back to the angels from where she had come,*
*A carpet of flowers strewn,*
*But you can see her from afar,*
*Looking down from heaven as a -*
                        *Brand new shining star.*

## Veronica Harding

## A Poem For Diana Princess Of Wales

*You were the Queen of my Heart,*
*But now you've gone to depart.*
*If only you could have known before,*
*How much we all love and adore,*
*You and all the work you've done,*
*And how you were a loving mum.*
*This was the most tragic end,*
*And now there are millions of hearts to mend.*
*We all did love you and now we must leave you,*
*Going to the place where nobody can touch you.*
*You understood children like me,*
*And now you have left, oh can't you see . . .*
*You were the Princess you were the Queen,*
*You were the other one, the one in-between,*
*You were the healer, you were the friend,*
*You were the helper who would never offend.*
*But most of all you were like darts*
*Firing love into people's hearts,*
*For you, Diana, Princess of Wales,*
*You, will always be the Queen of our Hearts.*

**Georgina Wise  (11)**

## England's Rose

Born first of July nineteen sixty one,
The life of Diana had only just begun.

Raised at Park House her brother and sisters
in tow,
They played with the future Princess and didn't
even know.

With the death of their grandfather they
moved away,
To an estate called Althorp where her family
did stay.

At the age of nineteen she met the
Prince of Wales,
This took place in Sussex amongst the hay bales.

On February twenty-fourth nineteen eighty one,
Was the date of their engagement known
by everyone.

St Pauls Cathedral was where their marriage
was to start,
Watched by the nation thrilled to the heart.

June twenty-first saw the birth of a son,
The people cried tears of joy for a new life
had begun.

His name was Prince William, an heir to
the throne,
In the eyes of the public he would become
well-known.

Three years later saw the arrival of another,
Prince William was finally to have a brother.

*Prince Harry was his name a second son of a proud mum and dad,*
*They knew he would grow to become a handsome young lad.*

*Diana was loved for her charity work in all parts,*
*That's how she became our Queen of Hearts.*

*Visiting victims of AIDS, Leprosy and land mines,*
*Laughing and joking making them shine.*

*Along came Dodi Al Fayed her last ever love,*
*The nation unaware that they were wanted*
*up above.*

*Then came the tragic day when Princess Di*
*bowed out,*
*The day the nation will never forget without a doubt.*

*Many felt the light had gone out of their hearts,*
*All the memories of her will never ever part.*

*Our thoughts are with Princes William and Harry on this day,*
*For the pain they feel in time will gradually*
*fade away.*

*Rest in peace Diana for the whole of the*
*nation knows,*
*On that fateful day we lost our English Rose.*

### Lisa Burgess of Handforth

## Diana

*Someone vital has left our lives but her presence*
*lingers on*
*Not just in the hearts of her friends and those who*
*knew her long,*
*But in the hearts of those whose lives she lifted with*
*a touch,*
*A word here and there, a gentle smile - that showed*
*us that she cared so much.*

*Maybe we were selfish and took all she had*
*to give;*
*We forgot that she was human too and had her life*
*to live.*
*We hounded her through kindness because we*
*wanted to know more*
*Of this lovely special lady and never really saw*
*That sometimes she was hurting too, that she felt*
*just the same*
*As those who could be lifted by the mention*
*of her name.*

*A young and caring Princess, Diana*
*was her name*
*Has given love to all the world which will never be*
*the same.*
*She taught us how to think of those who suffered so much more*
*Than we did - the sick, the sad, the poor.*
*We know that her heritage of love will never*
*ever cease,*
*And so, Princess of the People, may you always*
*Rest in Peace.*

**Maggie Pendaw**

## A Letter To Heaven

*Dear God up above*
*Tell Diana we send our love*
*Tell her here on Earth*
*We really cared*
*Wish she were here*
*So we could share*
*We never realised*
*The effect, she had*
*On our lives.*
*To bid her last farewell*
*Under a grieving spell*
*Strangers from other lands*
*Came hand-in-hand*
*United in their stand*
*For a Princess*
*Whom we all loved*
*Now with you  up above*
*Tell her, in our hearts*
*She will always remain*
*A Princess, friend*
*Who'll forever reign*
*Put your arms around her, Lord*
*Give her love and tender care*
*Something she would do*
*Were she still here*
*With a final adieu*
*We give our love to you.*
*With love and tender care*
      *From the people in despair.*

**N Healy**

## Diana

*A voice for all the voiceless ones -*
*The outcast and alone;*
*The homeless and rejected ones*
*You treated as your own.*
*There was no rank, there was no class,*
*Just people in their need.*
*You showed your care, you showed your love -*
*The 'Queen of Hearts' indeed.*

*Your touch restored humanity*
*To those we turned aside.*
*You showed what needed to be done*
*And all the risks defied.*
*From your own pain you comfort brought*
*And love in action showed,*
*And by your care to hurting ones*
*New self-esteem bestowed.*

*May we complete what you began*
*And seek that love to share,*
*Knowing that everyone on earth*
*Is worthy of our care.*
*The lessons from your so short life*
*May we be quick to learn.*
*May all our hearts, and all our lives*
*With that same passion burn.*

**A S Clifton**

### Diana, Princess Of Wales

*Where are you dear Diana,*
*Can you see the Nation cry,*
*Can you hear the anguished voices*
*Questioning 'Why?'*

*You did so much for many*
*In this harsh and hostile World,*
*With a look, a touch, a gesture,*
*Hope and love unfurled.*

*Our thoughts are with your family*
*They may help in some way,*
*But, Diana, Queen of Hearts,*
*In our hearts you'll always stay.*

*We hope you rest in peace now*
*Wherever you may be*
*And that somehow your work continues*
*Let Love be your Legacy.*

**A P Stevens**

## Diana

*Queen of Hearts, that's who you are,*
*now you're safely with the shining stars,*
*looking down at us, watching us all,*
*we will never forget you at all,*
*no-one can ever replace you Diana*
*for you are England's beautiful carer*
*we thank you, love you, miss you Diana*
*but mostly of course we'll never forget you.*
*Diana, Princess of Wales you are*
            *our England's rose.*

### Joanne & Nathan


## It Was A Tragic Parting

*It was a tragic parting*
*too tragic to forget.*
*Those who loved you dearly*
*are the ones who won't forget.*
*So we will hold you close within*
*our hearts, and there you will remain*
*to walk with us throughout our lives*
*until we meet again.*
*So rest in peace dear Diana and thanks*
*for all you've done.*
*Pray that God has given you*
*the crown you've truly won.*

### E Peel

## Forever Our Princess

The nation mourns,
for the loss of our Princess,
who in making lives happy,
had so much success.

Our friend has gone,
the grief we feel,
our silent despair,
will never ever heal.

A beautiful woman,
so strong yet so weak,
an amazing gift,
so kind, so unique.

Taken from us,
at such a young age,
leaving two boys,
with such heartache and rage.

What really happened?
It's so unfair,
now you are gone,
believe it, do we dare?

All the world's a stage,
beautifully you played your parts,
Diana, you truly were,
The queen of all our hearts.

Where do you walk now,
nobody knows,
but we will walk again with you,
goodbye for now, England's rose.

### Kelly White

## Diana - Flower Of England

*Princess Diana Flower of England your life's work*
*here is done*
*Drawn to an end so tragically with so many things*
*just begun*
*We stand aghast and tremble for no one can take*
*your place*
*Never more shall we see your majesty, your beauty*
*and your grace.*

*Oh Diana if you could but see, the nation brought*
*to tears*
*They cried for you, they cried for your boys and they*
*cried for your suffering years*
*And into your path they threw their hearts, they threw their flowers*
*and love*
*Not wanting to believe that you had been called to the Realms of*
*Glory above.*

*And the world looked on in numbness at our nation*
*washed in tears*
*As we paid our respects and bade you farewell at the*
*passing of your years*
*With us they too had witnessed, your compassion for*
*the sad and forlorn*
*Watched you reach out with love, to the castout, the*
*broken, the torn.*

*From deep within came the love that you gave, from a heart that*
*suffered so much*
*And to watch from afar was enough for us all, to feel your special*
*touch*
*And the nation knows a light has gone out, a light that lit up the*
*world*
*A light that will never be seen again, though eternity be unfurled.*

*You touched our hearts like no other could,*
*before you or beyond*
*You brought joy and happiness to all you held,*
*creating love's special bond*
*And that bond shall not be broken with the passing*
*of the years*
*It will grow and blossom and bear much fruit,*
*nurtured by a million tears.*

*God bless.*

### Colin & Margaret James

### Diana - The Mother

*She was a mum, just like me,*
*The love for her boys was plain to see.*
*Two boys with heads bowed low,*
*The nation sharing their sorrow.*
*Together they walked behind, on her final journey.*
*Flowers, a card, bearing one word 'Mummy'.*

*Watching the boys, their loss was so real,*
*I cannot imagine the ache they must feel.*
*The nation has lost a princess, a friend,*
*No-one really knows what happened at the end.*

*Boys, I hope the memories you cherish will ease*
                              *your pain,*
*And the love that surrounds you, will help you*
                              *smile once again.*

### Ann Elizabeth Hurley

## The People's Flower

From the tiniest of seeds a plant began to grow
Lovingly fed and watered, till leaves began to show.
Slowly pushing through the ground it started on
life's way
Tenderly loved and nurtured, protected every day.
Soon the floweret appeared, when from its
site profound
It was then transplanted out upon some strange
new ground.
Where its sweetness soon was seen by all who
passed it by
Hanging down its dainty head and looking oh so shy.
Then the plant was moved again although not far
from there
It seemed to thrive much better and gained a
beauty rare.
Anyone who ventured near when it was fully grown
Found themselves surrounded by a perfume
all its own.
Yet this place still wasn't right, which rather spoiled
the bloom,
It looked too overcrowded, in want of much
more room.
So once more the plant was moved this time to
foreign parts
And blossomed quite profusely, its name?
'The Queen of Hearts'.
Suddenly the stem was cut, that it would die
was plain,
But in the people's memory that flower will
still remain.

**Marie D Hollingworth**

## Diana

*Your respect for others*
*And your great sense of fun,*
*For the hearts of this nation*
*You certainly won.*

*The sadness inside*
*Didn't stand in your way*
*And the obstacles and heartaches*
*Didn't keep you at bay.*

*Visiting dying people around the world,*
*You touched their souls,*
*You inspired and loved them*
*Which gave them hope for their goals.*

*A shining example,*
*Though insecure yourself inside,*
*And the stripping of your HRH title,*
*Opened the photographers' gates wide.*

*The harassment which followed,*
*Finally led to your death,*
*We just didn't believe it and we*
*Took a great breath.*

*The week that followed*
*Of the shallow and the blamed,*
*Bowed their heads*
*For your life that they claimed.*

*But you will never be forgotten*
*And we'll rise up and carry a banner,*
*And spread just one word that means so much*
*And that is 'Diana!'*

**Debbie Twine**

## Diana

D iana, you lit up our lives,
I n helping others to survive.
A n endless smile and deep concern,
N o-one but you could make heads turn.
A bundant was the care you gave,

P assing crowds to whom you'd wave.
R emembering the down-at-heel,
I nviting ill your hands to feel.
N ow you are gone our lives seem bare,
C an we cope now you're not there.
E ven though you're laid to rest,
S omehow you'll always be the best.
S adness fills the world around,

O n that sad day there was no sound.
F aithful people, heads bowed low,

W eeping as you passed by slow.
A lthough you've gone, you are still here,
L ove won't leave you do not fear.
E ach day we'll still remember you,
S o rest in peace, we all love you.

**Gill Ward**

### Diana

*Princess of life*
*A lady of love*
*With hands of hope*
*Spreading peace . . .*

*'Thou art, our white dove'*

*Innocence, grace*
*and a childlike smile*
*You've captured us all*
*with your beauty and style.*

*The work that you've done*
*and breath that you gave . . .*
*the sick and the wounded*
*those lives you have saved.*

*Two people in love*
*in peace, you'll remain,*
*for eternal embrace*

*'at last'*

*In the Palace of Heaven . . .*
*OUR QUEEN will reign.*

**Amanda Southern**

## Heart-Rending

*You have passed through time*
*Diana, touched hearts like mine.*
*Your beauty, always to be young*
*Your mission just begun.*
*To those who struggled in need*
*You reached with heart-warming deeds.*
*A touch, a smile*
*Oh so fragile.*
*Simply to do good*
*You were often misunderstood*
*Flashing white lights stripped you bare*
*Your heart was only to care.*
*Your dignity assured*
*The Royal Standard flag caressed*
*The People's Princess.*
*Now you rest with heaven's best.*
*The People's Princess, Queen of Hearts*

**Anthony Keyes**


## A Tribute To Diana

*On this last day of August, nineteen ninety seven*
*Lovely Princess Diana, was sent up to heaven*
*There's a hush everywhere, in the towns and the vales*
*Everyone's mourning, our Princess of Wales.*

*Gracious compassionate, full of humility*
*She strived to help others, to the best of her ability*
*Without any warning, struck down in her prime*
*She won't be forgotten, she's a saint of her time.*

*We'll always remember, her kindness and empathy*
*To the sick and the needy, she showed them*
                                        *her sympahty*
*An Ambassador for Britain, and example*
                                        *to womanhood*
*Giving her time humbly, doing nothing but good.*

**Sheila Ware**


## Dodi And Di

*Dodi and Di, now departed*
*So many people left broken-hearted,*
*Why did it happen? No-one knows*
*But at least together are their souls.*
*Up in Heaven high above*
*No more pain, but so much love*
*Together now they are free*
*Happy so happy as they can be.*
*Away from people spying and prying*
*Are they the cause of their dying?*
*So many hearts are left broken*
*So many words left unspoken*
*For both their families, we must pray*
*Their memories of them will always stay.*

*My love to both families,*

**Julie Mahoney**

## God's Flower

When Diana walked thru the Heavenly gate
She told the Press there 'You can wait.'
God He knew for sure
Diana wanted to see the poor.
She gave a little frown
I am ordinary, I don't need a crown.
The angels cheered from their cloud
They were so very proud.
She wanted to help God, could tell
'Let's visit the poor down in Hell.'
God used His magic power
To make a special flower.
And the name He chose
He called it His English Rose.

**Colin Allsop**


## Diana 1961-1997
## On This Day August 31st '97

On this day
   Diana died.
On this day,
   The world it cried.

On this day,
   The world stood still.
On this day
   You left a gap
No-one else can fill.

On this day,
  No-one could believe,
The entire, overwhelming,
  Shock we feel.

On this day
  A woman of substance,
Passed on by
  All we can do,
Is sit and cry.

**Andrea Edwards**


## The Blooming Of A Rose

In the shade of the realm was a rosebud so shy
Which slowly blossomed, catching our eye
An innocent bloom - a true English rose
With such beauty, everybody knows
Full of compassion a quality rare
For the sick and the poor she really did care
Her inner beauty outwardly showed
Surrounded by an aura she positively glowed
Poise and serenity this rose did possess
Showing love for us all - the people's princess
Though some of her days were often grey
Dutifully she smiled, hiding dismay
But this princess - on earth - had too few years
We mourn her loss and still shed our tears
Now in heaven's garden she eternally grows
Princess Diana - our English rose.

**Val Farrell**

## Diana 1961-1997

*To a very special lady,*
*Whose smile never ended,*
*Whose tears never lied,*
*Whose thoughts and happiness was always shared,*
*Whose love was for all,*
*Someone who cared and spoke from her heart*
*To the people of the nation, the people of the world,*
*Through the good times and the bad - she always*
*Came through,*
*Her loving nature and beautiful smile that*
*Will always be remembered and will never die,*
*Her spirit will live on forever,*
*Goodnight sweet lady,*
       *Diana - Princess of Wales.*

**Victoria Mitchell**


## Untitled

*Diana, Princess of Wales,*
*a real life princess in fairy tales,*
*With your heart and soul you always cared,*
*with so much enthusiasm you forever shared,*
*Comforting all those with troubles and strife,*
*you accomplished so much in such a short life,*
*Loving your sons, Princes Harry and William,*
*We all agree you were a mum in a million,*
*The whole country will mourn and shed many tears,*
*The pain and the loss we shall feel for years,*
*Diana and Dodi are now laid to rest,*
*Why is it God only takes the best?*

**The Hutchinson Family**

## Our Queen Of Hearts

*This is a very sad day*
*For people everywhere*
*Princess Diana died today*
*With the man who really cared*
*They are both together now*
*No man can ever part*
*She cared for everyone here*
*She was our Queen of Hearts*
*She cared for the sick and for the poor*
*People with AIDS and many more*
*We pray for her sons she left behind*
*And hope they will be given peace*
*We pray the laws will now be changed*
*And paparazzi will eventually cease*
*We know she is still living on*
*Working from heaven above*
*She is still looking down on us*
*And sending all her love*
*So let's give thanks for her short life*
*The life an angel brings*
*She's holding hands with our Lord*
*As He gives her, her deserving wings*
*Today we feel sad so very sad*
*And I will tell you why*
*Today we lost a very dear friend*
*We lost our precious Di.*

**Linda Field**

## A Pain So Deep

A pain so deep, it's rarely felt,
Hearts are broken, stood weeping tears,
A light blown out, no longer there the ice to melt.

A people's princess she was to one and all,
A love so strong it glowed all around,
So genuine and caring she stood tall.

Elegance and beauty with a heart of gold,
A special friend to those she knew,
Kind and caring never would she be bought or sold.

Two precious sons she gave to us all,
To follow in her footsteps, to be strong and lead,
They will carry on the kindness and goodwill
                                    never to fall.

The end it came too soon, to bring her peace of
                                    the white dove,
An eternal flame to glow in our hearts,
Gone forever now our Princess in an endless love.

To rest at last without the cameras haunting,
Total privacy for evermore, no need for running,
Where she has gone there will be no more taunting.

**Rebecca Simmonds**

## Goodbye Sweet Princess

*Your timeless beauty, your ardent grace*
*You helped to make this world a beautiful place*
*The words of comfort, the hands you held,*
*Your light shone bright around the world.*

*From the rich and famous to the layman and poorer*
*We have all been blessed by your healing aura.*
*Can this world endure such tragedy,*
*When it was you alone that gave such clarity.*

*Our Queen of Hearts, our sister friend,*
*Will our sadness ever end?*
*Is there a soul on earth, that didn't love her?*
*Could you have been our 'Holy Mother'?*

*Forgive our ignorance of the past*
*Of that we may never alter*
*As Venus be the goddess of Love, you must*
                    *surely be her daughter.*
*Amongst the angels in Heaven, your star*
                    *will shine the best*
*Goodbye sweet Princess, may your soul be at rest.*

### Jacqui Green

## Our Diana

Tears on my pillow, I cried each night
The world has lost its guiding light
You showed the world how to love and care
For God to take you away, it's not fair
For the children it was to be hugged or kissed
By them alone you will be sadly missed
For those who suffered you gave your tender touch
To others your smile meant so much
A nation mourns a loss of a special treasure
For me to have known you would have been
                                  a pleasure
Our Diana is now at rest
The world she is in must be the best
The human race must continue Diana's fight
To stop suffering, wars, and put things right.
With broken hearts, so full of sorrows
Never, never, forget our Diana in our tomorrows.

**Rowan Lee**

# INFORMATION

We hope you have enjoyed reading this book - and that you will continue to enjoy it in the coming years.

If you like reading and writing poetry drop us a line, or give us a call, and we'll send you a free information pack.

Write to :-
**Arrival Press Information**
**1-2 Wainman Road**
**Woodston**
**Peterborough**
**PE2 7BU**
**(01733) 230762**